Vagabond
Witness

Victor Serge and the politics of hope

Paul Gordon

Winchester, UK
Washington, USA

First published by Zero Books, 2013
Zero Books is an imprint of John Hunt Publishing Ltd., Laurel House, Station Approach,
Alresford, Hants, SO24 9JH, UK
office1@jhpbooks.net
www.johnhuntpublishing.com
www.zero-books.net

For distributor details and how to order please visit the 'Ordering' section on our website.

Text copyright: Paul Gordon 2012

ISBN: 978 1 78099 327 0

A CIP catalogue record for this book is available from the British Library.

Design: Stuart Davies

Printed and bound by CPI Group (UK) Ltd, Croydon, CR0 4YY

We operate a distinctive and ethical publishing philosophy in all
areas of our business, from our global network of authors to
production and worldwide distribution.

CONTENTS

For John Berger
with love and gratitude

'What does not change / is the will to change'
Charles Olson, 'The Kingfishers'

Acknowledgements

This book simply would not have come into being without Gareth Evans. Love and thanks to him and to Melissa Benn and Graham Music for their encouragement and critical engagement; also to Hannah and Sarah, for being who they are. If I may borrow some words from Serge, I am grateful to them all for existing.

The music of Dino Saluzzi and Mal Waldron, brooding, tender, searching, endlessly evocative, provided the perfect soundtrack.

Paul Gordon
July 2012

Permissions
The quotations from Serge's novels are used by kind permission of the translator, Richard Greeman. The lines from Serge's poems are reprinted by kind permission of City Lights Books, translation (c) 1989 by James Brook. The lines from 'The Kingfishers' are from Charles Olson, *The Collected Poems of Charles Olson, Excluding the Maximus Poems*. (c) 1987 by the Regents of the University of California, reprinted by kind permission of the University of California Press.

Victor Serge - a life line

1890 - Born 30 December, Victor Lvovich Kibalchich, into Russian revolutionary émigré family in Brussels

1912 - Sentenced to five years in French prison for association with armed anarchist gang

1915 - Marries Rirette Maitrejean

1917 - Released from prison, takes part in syndicalist uprising in Barcelona
Russian Revolution

1918 - Interned in concentration camp in France trying to get to Russia

1919 - Arrives in Petrograd to join the revolution, marries Liuba Russakova

1920 - Son, Vlady, born

1923 - Comintern agent in Berlin and Vienna

1924 - Death of Lenin, succession of Stalin

1928 - Expelled from Communist Party, begins writing fiction, *Men in Prison* (1930), *Birth of our Power* (1930) and *Conquered City* (1932), all published in France

1933 - Exiled to Orenburg, near Kazakhstan, writes *Midnight in the Century* (1939) and much of his poetry

1935 - Daughter, Jeannine, born

1936 - International solidarity campaign secures his exit from Soviet Union, lives in Brussels and Paris

1937 - Publishes *Destiny of a Revolution* and *From Lenin to Stalin*

1940 - Fall of France; assassination of Trotsky in Coyocoan, Mexico

1941 - Begins exile in Mexico where he writes three more novels, *The Long Dusk*, *The Case of Comrade Tulayev* and *Unforgiving Years*, and *Memoirs of a Revolutionary*, marries Laurette Sejourne

1947 - Dies of heart attack, 17 November, stateless, he is buried as a Spaniard in the French cemetery

Introduction:

the art of not dying away

Dazzling. That was the last word Victor Serge ever wrote. In his poem, 'Hands', a meditation on a sixteenth century terra cotta, which he had finished and typed up in the early hours of the day that would be his last. That evening, Tuesday 17 November 1947, he had gone out to see his artist son, Vlady, but he wasn't at home. He met Julian Gorkin, his old comrade, who had traveled from revolutionary Barcelona to greet him in Brussels when he was finally allowed to leave Russia. They talked for a bit before shaking hands and parting. Probably feeling unwell, he decided to take a cab home. His heart gave way before he even had time to tell the driver where he wanted to go.

Gorkin went to the police station to identify him just after midnight:

> In a bare shabby room with grey walls, he was laid out on an old operating table, wearing a threadbare suit and a worker's shirt, with holes in his shoes. A cloth bandage covered the mouth that all the tyrannies of the century had not been able to shut. One might have thought him a vagabond who had been taken in out of charity. In fact, had he not been an eternal vagabond of life in search of the ideal? His face still bore the stamp of bitter irony, an expression of protest...[1]

He had arrived here six years before with Vlady - his companion, Laurette, and his daughter, Jeannine, would come later - fleeing from Nazi-occupied Europe, leaving behind a lifetime of political activity - an anarchist in France, a syndicalist in Spain, a critical Bolshevik in Russia, an agent of the Comintern in Germany and Austria, years of internal exile in Russia, a supporter of the revolutionary POUM in Spain, of which Gorkin had been one of the leaders. The journey had taken six months on a cargo ship he described as 'an ersatz concentration camp of the sea'. There were more than 300 of them on it, including the surrealist Andre Breton, with whom Serge had campaigned in Paris against the Stalinist show-trials, and Breton's wife, Jacqueline. Oddly, the passengers included the anthropologist Claude Levi-Strauss, on his way to a new post in New York. Levi-Strauss was clearly in awe of Serge: he was a man, after all, who had known Lenin, but he found his physical presence at odds with his preconceptions. 'more like an elderly and spinster aunt ... with an asexual quality ... very far removed from the virile and superabundant vitality commonly associated ... with subversive activities.' This, surely, says more about Levi-Strauss than it does about Serge. (Although he complained, Levi-Strauss traveled in comparative comfort compared to most of the passengers, as he was one of the few to have the use of the ship's two cabins.)

By stark contrast, the young man who would become Mexico's greatest writer and who would eventually win the Nobel Prize, Octavio Paz, had met Serge in Paris not long before and was 'immediately and powerfully' drawn to him. 'I spent hours talking with him, 'he recalled. 'Serge's human warmth, his directness and generosity, could not have been further from the pedantry of the dialecticians. A moist intelligence. In spite of his sufferings, setbacks. and long years of arid political arguments, he had managed to preserve his humanity. ... I was not moved by his ideas, but by his person ... an example of the fusion of two opposing qualities: moral and intellectual intransigence with tolerance and compassion.' (It was Serge who introduced Paz to the work of the French painter/writer, Henri Michaux, 'a discovery of capital importance for me'.)[2]

Their journey involved yet another period in prison (this time in French-run Martinique) and, then bizarrely, his first ever flight in a plane. Mexico was not his choice but there was nowhere else, and it had become a home of sorts to thousands of political refugees, thanks to Lazaro Cardenas, the former president whose government was one of the few to have supported the Republican side in Spain, and opened the country to many Spanish and other exiles.

But the exiles brought their disputes with them, and these were often violent. Only a few months before Serge got there, Trotsky had finally fallen to the assassins who had pursued him for so long. (A previous attempt had involved an armed raid on his compound led by the Communist artist David Siqueiros, who would eventually find refuge in Chile, thanks to the intervention of the Chilean consul-general in Mexico, a poet who would come in time to speak for thousands in his hatred of oppression, one Pablo Neruda. Strange days indeed.)

Serge's and Gorkin's own lives were threatened and on more than one occasion they had to go into hiding. The country's president received appeals from US and British politicians and intellectuals calling on him to protect them. At the same time, the editor of a magazine to which they had contributed was being told by the Interior Minister, Miguel Aleman, later to be President, that the governments of Britain and the USSR were demanding that all platform be withdrawn from these 'agents of Hitler'. Meetings were broken up and, on one occasion, Gorkin and another comrade were stabbed.

Always poor, and often indescribably lonely, (as he wrote to a friend), he explored the country. And he wrote and wrote and wrote - for *Partisan Review, Politics, Horizon, New Leader* (as their Mexican correspondent), *The New International, Mundo, Libertad y Socialismo*. And three more novels: his best, his most ambitious yet, against all the odds to add to the four he'd already published, *The Long Dusk, The Case of Comrade Tulayev* and *Unforgiving Years*. And a life of Trotsky with his widow, Natalia Zedova, a real act of generosity given Trotsky's abuse of Serge when he had dared to disagree. Only one of these would be published while he was still alive. Writing for the desk drawer, he called it.

With characteristic lack of self-pity, Serge wrote in his notebook: 'It is terribly difficult to create in a void without the slightest support, without the least ambience ... at the age of 50 ... facing an unknown future which does not exclude the possibility that the dictatorships will last longer than the rest of my life.' And he was living at an altitude, over 7,000 ft above sea-level, that could do him no good whatsoever because of his heart, and learning to live with endless *temblores* (earthquakes), 2000 recorded each year.

And he read and read, making sense of the world as the ever worse news reached him from Europe. And he developed his interest in psychology. He'd always believed in the soul, what Vlady called his 'materialist spirituality'. This interest was encouraged by his friendship with the revolutionary German psychiatrists, Fritz Fraenckel and Hubert Lennhof. He was grief struck by Fraenckel's early death - he was only 52 - in June 1943, and it was a year before he was able to write about him, forcing himself to do so, knowing 'only too well the frailty of memory and the iniquitous and impoverishing omission which entombs the dead'. 'I owe a great deal,' Serge wrote, to his 'intelligent equilibrium in a time of instability and to his intellectual richness, which the malicious and the foolish weren't able to appreciate on account of his ways as an amused, sad and irresolute Bohemian ... 'How light he was on the earth!' At his funeral Serge said, 'Nobody who came close to him escaped his influence, everyone has been made at least a little better.' (Lennhof whispered, 'You don't know how much hostility there was towards him.')

And it was here in exile that Serge wrote his single, greatest work, the incomparable *Memoirs of a Revolutionary*, a work of political witness and engagement and solidarity, unparalleled since. The very first lines speak of a deep feeling he had known from childhood, of 'living in a world without any possible escape, in which there was nothing for it but to fight for an impossible escape'. (The very same existentialist dilemma was being articulated thousands of miles away by Sartre, Camus and de Beauvoir ...)

Looking back on his life, Serge said:

I give myself credit for having seen clearly in a number of important situations. In itself, this is not so difficult to achieve, and yet it is rather unusual. To my mind, it is less a question of an exalted or shrewd intelligence, than of good sense, goodwill and a certain sort of courage to enable one to rise above the pressures of one's environment and the natural inclination to close one's eyes to facts, a temptation that arises from our immediate interests and from the fear which problems inspire in us.

Among the countless things he had seen clearly: that the creation of the Cheka (the secret police) in 1917 was one of the Bolsheviks' 'gravest and most impermissible errors'; that the Bolshevik leadership had lied about the nature of the Kronstadt rebellion in 1921; that the Communists would turn on the independent revolutionary left in Spain; that Stalin would eliminate the entire 1917 revolutionary generation in order to safeguard his power; that Russia had become a vast prison camp. (It was Serge who first described the state as totalitarian.)

And yet he never lost hope, that ordinary people would act for themselves and take control of their own lives. On the ship taking him away from Europe he recalled, 'The Russians and Spaniards among us know what it is to take the world into their hands, to set the railways running and the factories working ... no kind of predestination impels us to become the offal of the concentration camps.' He wasn't one of those former communists, whose 'god had failed', for he had never had one. For him there was no inevitability in how the revolution had turned out, any more than there was inevitability in anything. History was made by men and women who made choices.

Hoping to return to Europe, Serge envisaged a democratic renewal, 'of traditional democratic freedoms made revolutionary once again', in order 'simply to practice the art of not dying away'.

* * *

It would be wrong to suggest that Serge was completely unrecognized during his life. Far from it; it was precisely his standing internationally that protected him from Stalin and brought about his and his immediate family's release from the Soviet Union, although it could not save his remaining relatives, most of whom would die in camps.[3] And, because he wrote in French, several of his novels and his poetry were published in France, although obviously not in Russia. (One, *Midnight in the Century*, was even nominated for the Prix Goncourt, the prestigious French literary prize, in 1939, although it didn't win.)

And he had his influential admirers and supporters who included the radical US critic and editor, Dwight Macdonald, and George Orwell, who tried to find a publisher for his *Memoirs*. (Serge was so poor he had only one copy of the manuscript which he was, understandably, reluctant to trust to the transatlantic mail.) And he is even a character in a poem 'Aesthetique du mal', by Wallace Stevens. The first of his books to be translated into English, *The Long Dusk*, was translated by Ralph Manheim, who would go on to become the foremost translator of contemporary German writers, including Brecht and Gunter Grass. And, in Britain, some of his books were published in mass-market editions by Penguin in the 1960s.

But since his death his work has had a precarious existence, going in and out of print, and waiting a long time to be translated into English. While *The Long Dusk* was translated by Ralph Manheim the year before Serge died, all his other novels waited a long time. It was 20 years before Roger Trask's translation of *The Case of Comrade Tulayev* appeared. Richard Greeman's translations of *Men in Prison, Birth of Our Power* and *Conquered City* all appeared in the early 1970s. But it was a further ten years before *Midnight in the Century* appeared in translation, with *Unforgiving Years* doing so only in 2008, nearly sixty years after it was written. And while the *Memoirs* were published in 1963 by Oxford University Press in Peter Sedgwick's pellucid translation, they insisted he cut the manuscript by one-eighth before they would do so. It is only now, nearly 50 years later in 2012, that we have a complete English version. (Richard Greeman tells the story of Sedgwick's labors, an act of love and of solidarity, in the new edition.)

And since his death he has, of course, had his prominent partisans. His 'unrepentant humanism' was celebrated by Christopher Hampton in his quietly thoughtful book, *Socialism in a Crippled World* (1981), while Christopher Hitchens acknowledged him as 'the first person to recognize and comprehend the roots of the emerging Stalinist regime'. For John Berger, there is 'no other writer with whom Serge can very usefully be compared'. This singularity, for Berger, the 'essence of the man and his books', is to be found in his attitude to the truth; 'for Serge the value of the truth extended far beyond the simple (or complex) telling of it ... The truth for Serge was something to be undergone.' In her introduction to a new edition of *The Case of Comrade Tulayev*, Susan Sontag was moved to a generous celebration of the man:

> There was nothing, ever, triumphant about his life ... except[s] the triumph of being immensely gifted and industrious as a writer ... of being principled and also astute and ... incapable of keeping company with the faithful and cravenly gullible ...

of being incorruptible as well as brave and therefore on a lonely, different path from the liars and toadies and careerists, the triumph of being, after the 1920s, right.[4]

But Serge has also been the subject of almost casual misrepresentation: the maverick British Trotskyite, David Widgery, dedicated his impressive account of the left in Britain to his memory, describing him as a 'Syndicalist, Bolshevik, Trotskyist', conveniently forgetting the anarchist he had been for many years, which got him several years in prison and which was *always* part of who he was, while the epithet 'Trotskyist' is just misleading. A biography of the 'American Pimpernel', Varian Fry, who helped Serge and very many other intellectuals and artists to escape from France in 1940, describes him as a man 'who had travelled the revolutionary road from violence to tolerance', a gross oversimplification, that is also a misrepresentation. And it's a surprise to see the radical, and usually inspired, critic, John Leonard, say of him, that he 'had helped the Russian Revolution but then run away from it'. Really? Serge didn't run from anything, other than the Nazis in 1940 when his life and the lives of his family were in danger and he had done everything he could to put the revolution right, or at least stop it going wrong.[5] And even Sontag, in what is otherwise a marvelous appreciation of the man, somehow manages to depoliticize him, which is quite a feat, given that he was born, lived and died a political being. It is this, more than anything else, that has stopped him getting the recognition that is his due. And while we must be grateful to the individuals and groups on the far left who have done so much to keep Serge's words and spirit alive, he is much too important to be a figure of the margins.

* * *

For myself, I first read Victor Serge as a disaffected teenager in the late 1960s/early 1970s, when I was trying to make sense of this thing called communism which seemed to be doing such terrible things in the world, despite its claim to be acting for the benefit of humankind, an idea to which I was strongly drawn. One of the books on our shelves at home was a volume called *The God That Failed*, a collection of essays by former Communists, about why they had become disillusioned. The book, edited by the Labour MP Richard Crossman, with contributions by Richard Wright, Ignazio Silone and Arthur Koestler and others, was a popular volume with a catchy title, that seemed to damn the communist cause pretty conclusively. Equally damning were books like Alexander Solzhenitsyn's *One Day in the Life of Ivan Denisovich*, Koestler's *Darkness at Noon*, and George Orwell's *Animal Farm* and *Nineteen Eighty Four*, which I read around the same time. It was at the same time that I came across Serge's, *The Case of Comrade Tulayev*, then published in its iconic Modern Classics series by Penguin. But this was telling a much more subtle and complex story that I was only able to appreciate with time.

Serge's *Memoirs* is the book I've read more often, and given to more people, than any other. Many people will recognize themselves in Serge biographer Susan Weissman's account of her total absorption. She first read them on a long train journey but had not finished them when she reached her destination. She sat on a bench in the station and read right to the end. Even after many readings, I still have to tear myself away once I pick them up, they are so engrossing. It was also one of the books I took traveling with me after I left university, including to Portugal, then in the throes of its own revolution, along with the wonderful Penguin volume of John Berger's *Selected Essays*, and John Dos Passos' massive *USA*, an astonishing counter-story of that country's development. (I learned much later that Serge admired Dos Passos and was clearly influenced by him.)

I have never had a need for heroes, but Serge is a man I have

admired greatly for most of my life and my admiration has
deepened with my reading and re-reading of him over the years.
That he wrote at all given the circumstances of his life, the persecution and the poverty, is remarkable; that he wrote so creatively,
tellingly, movingly, is little short of astonishing, as is the fact that
he never lost hope that people could take their destiny in their
own hands and make a better world. And I've always loved the
fact that this man - novelist, poet, historian, witness, revolutionary activist, humanist - who spoke several languages, never
set foot inside an institution of formal learning; his father thought
it 'stupid bourgeois instruction for the poor'. He was truly
educated in museums, libraries and churches and in 'ransacking
encyclopedias' and in, what he calls somewhere, 'the university
of the streets'.

* * *

So what follows is an introduction to a man who really shouldn't
need it and who, in many ways, does not; all we have to do,
ultimately, is to read him. But he does need to be contextualized
and that is what I've done, as well as provide a critical appreciation of his main writings, following, roughly, the chronology of
his novels. If I've quoted him at length in places that's because he
says things so much better than any paraphrase or summary and
also because he often achieves what he does by an accumulation
of images. (That's why I quote rarely from the *Memoirs*; as
someone said, the problem in writing about Serge's life is that he
says it all so much better than we can.) And, yes, this is also a
celebration of a unique and inspiring man and repayment of a
debt of gratitude that is long overdue.

In the shadow of madness: the experience of prison

'I was no longer a man', Serge wrote of the moment of sentence, but 'a man in prison. An inmate'. The process of dehumanization started then, 'I had crossed the invisible boundary'. Admission to the prison itself began with the inmates losing their few personal effects, 'We start out by being robbed.' And whatever individuality they have is also taken away when their heads are shaved and they are 'sufficiently depersonalized' to appear before the administrative authorities. Nothing distinguishes one man from another, 'the same stubbly chins, the same shaved skulls - and doubtless the same look of the hunted man'. The mass photographing, 'a gallery of lost souls', further reduces every one to two or three varieties of expression: 'animal passivity, confusion, humiliation - each modified by anger, despair, defiance, or taciturn sullenness ...'

When he was in his early twenties, Victor Serge was implicated by the French police in the activities of the notorious 'Bonnot Gang', a group of illegalist anarchists who had been causing havoc in parts of the country. Believers in the 'propaganda of the deed', they carried out armed robberies and made their getaway by car, which was then something of a novelty. Serge had expressed his support for them and when police raided the offices of the newspaper he edited, they found a couple of revolvers. He refused to give evidence against the robbers, was convicted and given what could only be seen as a vindictive sentence of five years imprisonment. Writing nearly 30 years later, Serge wrote, with an honesty and self-evident pain, of the emotional legacy this had left him:

It burdened me with an experience so heavy, so intolerable to endure, that long afterwards, when I resumed writing, my first book (a novel) amounted to an effort to free myself from this inward nightmare, as well as performing a duty towards all those who will never so free themselves ...

Although written in the first person, narrated by a man who is never named, *Men in Prison* is, Serge makes clear at the outset, a work of fiction, but it is also true. 'Everything in this book is fictional and everything is true.' Serge said that what he was trying to do, was through literary creation, to bring out the general meaning and human contents of a personal experience. In other words, Serge is saying, don't make the mistake of thinking that this book, is about me. The book is called, after all, *men* in prison, not *a man* in prison. It's about all men 'crushed in that dark corner of society'. And the only way open to Serge to do it at that time, with the creative resources available to him, was as a first person narrative. He was being true to his own experience, but also that of the many people whose lives he had shared or observed.

The rules of the prison can be summarized, Serge wrote, in three peremptory words: *'Living is forbidden!'* Everything in prison came down to this. Above all, life was extinguished through time. Prisoners often speak of 'doing time'. They are punished through the theft of time; it is not theirs and what time there is, is either structured, as in meaningless work, or dead, empty time that destroys the soul. Serge was able to articulate this with an emotional depth which is truly frightening. Faced with 'the mystery of time's passage', the experience of time becomes like a torture. There are minutes and hours which have no end, 'the eternity of the instant'. But there are also empty hours, endless days, and weeks which pass without 'leaving the least memory behind them, as if they had never been. I cannot distinguish the years that are behind me'.

When they are repeated indefinitely, the same feelings grow dull. One loses count of the hours and the days. Even something that moved or terrified during the first days no longer has any effect: 'Suffocation? Drowning? A torpor sneaks into your veins, between your temples: All of life takes on the faded ocher-hue of the cell. You can no more escape this torpor than you can escape these four walls. The rhythm of your inner life slows down.'

Night brings no respite:

Even the city's rumble seems to have stopped. Nothing. Sleep is impossible ... I am already in a sort of tomb. I can do nothing. I see, hear, and feel nothing. I only know the next hour will be exactly like this one. The contrast between this vacant, empty prison time and the intense rhythms of normal life is so violent that it will take a long and painful adaptation to slow down the pulse of life, to deaden the will, to stifle, blot out, obliterate every unsettling image from my mind.

This experience comes to feel like being buried, a terrifying sensation that occurs again and again in the book: 'Burial. Each hour is like a shovelful of earth falling noiselessly, softly, on this grave ... I am alone in a numbered sepulchre ... Stretched out on my cot, like a dead man in his shroud (I even like to cross my hands over my chest like a dead man) ...'[6]

Life is also extinguished through hard work, forced labor, 'poured onto the limit of your strength', twelve hours a day, from seven in the morning to seven in the evening. Not only that, but this work was supposed to be done in absolute, perpetual silence. The absurdity of that rule was, Serge commented, equaled only by its cruelty. 'If it were actually enforced and respected, it would be the simplest way to drive the prisoners quietly mad'. In practice, it was not rigidly applied, but its very existence gave the guards huge power as they could resort to it as and when they wanted, at any moment.

The prison also did all it could to kill any living relationship between prisoners. Communication between the inmates, as in the use of the 'telephone', using the wastepipes of the building, was especially severely punished. But even something as banal as whistling, humming, talking to yourself out loud were prohibited, as these too were signs of life, however pathetic. Of course, prisoners disobeyed, but they did so in a situation of considerable fear that they would be caught.

Serge was an acute observer of how the modern prison *as a building* served its function beautifully. The only 'perfect and irreproachable work of architecture in the modern city', he said, its perfection lay in the total subordination of its design to its function: 'Its perfection is revealed at first glance: it is impossible to mistake it for any other kind of edifice. It is proudly, insularly, itself.' It was able to do the seemingly impossible task of housing a vast crowd, while achieving the total isolation of each individual in that crowd: 'Busier than a beehive, it is able to accomplish, silently and systematically, as many different tasks as there are lives tossed into its grinding cogs'.

The hold of the modern, urban prison was total. No one ever escaped from them. While people even used to escape from the Bastille, that symbol of pre-revolutionary despotism, and even from the French overseas territories of New Caledonia and Guiana, where people were transported, 'no one escapes from the model jail'.

Serge resisted completely any tendency to romanticize his fellow prisoners. One encountered, he remarked, just the same proportion of 'weak spirits, human scum, average types, and exceptional men, gifted with some spark of divinity', as anywhere else. As for the warders, they too, he said, were criminal, but respectably so, and with a guaranteed immunity from punishment for anything they might do. These people, who included 'sadists, inflexible hypocrites, morons, racketeers', could look forward to a pension at the end of their unspeakable lives. Serge drew a devastating picture of this person:

> The hybrid of bureaucratic scribbler and turnkey ... a singu-
> larly monotonous breed ... their bodies grown fat from sitting
> ... faces ... stamped by the murky grayness of the prison
> bureau ... eyes ... grown dim with the horrid dullness that
> emanates from the forms, receipts, registers and filing
> cabinets, where the same inanely bureaucratic descriptions of
> hopeless victims and miserable wretches pile up *ad
> infinitum*...

And yet, 'incredible as it may seem', there were also warders
who were good and 'almost intelligent', men who were capable
of acts of kindness, when, for instance, they would respond to
the pleadings of a man in isolation who is 'too weary of solitude',
and allow him a yard companion during exercise. On one such
occasion, the narrator himself met a man who, when hearing he
was an anarchist, shook his hand effusively. This man had
known Peter Kropotkin and Pierre Martin, prominent Russian
and French anarchists respectively, who had signed the 1883
Manifesto of the Anarchists and been imprisoned for their
politics.

The warders and inmates ended up in a bizarre, shared
existence, 'the same life on both sides of the same bolted door'.
(The use of the familiar *tu*, as a form of address, was evidence of
an instinctive recognition of a common existence and a common
mentality.) And yet, of course, warders had power and prisoners
were powerless; few men in modern society, Serge observed,
wielded 'such absolute power' over their fellow men as did
prison wardens. They had, in effect the power of life and death
over the prisoner:

> All it takes from him is a suggestion to the chief Guard ... and
> the prisoner ... is constantly harassed with petty discipline

and loaded down with penalties. The Warden can inflict penalties up to ninety days in the hole; more than enough to send the man ... to the infirmary, eyes ruined, lungs ravaged by tuberculosis, throat swollen, and ears dripping pus ... in effect, several sentences of slow death ...

Those disciplined were subjected to an extremely harsh regime, with their rations reduced to dry bread and morning soup; they have to march for twenty minutes with their arms folded across their chests, then for twenty minutes with their arms folded behind their backs. Even when they are allowed to rest, they have to sit with their legs together, their elbows pressed to their sides. They marched 30 miles a day.

Every man who is thrown into a cell, Serge said, immediately begins to live 'in the shadow of madness'. Serge was an acute observer of the many ways in which people fended off this ever-present threat. Something as unremarkable as walking was something everyone discovered within a few hours of being inside, 'He begins to walk', he says simply. Some, like him, even write poems as they do so. Others, like the narrator too, turned to books, but the bulk of the prison library consisted of bad adventure novels, probably bought because not even the public would buy them, but then there was also a collection of Balzac, 'heaven-sent'. At breaks in work everyone would read, but some books had to be disguised so as to appear as if they came from the library. A strange type of contraband came into existence, for which the prisoners even invented a word, *camelote*, such as a volume of Casanova's Memoirs, while the narrator reads the philosopher, Taine, on intelligence. Each, in its own way, provides 'rich spiritual nourishment'.

Serge would also say later that it was the possibility of writing about his experience that helped keep him sane. As he wrote to his friend, the Romanian writer Panait Istrati, 'I already saw a kind of justification of that infernal voyage in the possibility of describing it'.

Visits from families, too, helped men survive, but these, also, could be a source of torment, loaded with a weight of expectation they could not possibly bear, accompanied by shame and embarrassment. People were unable to touch each other, but there were times too when, because of the darkness, people could not even see each other clearly. *'The other person is there*: corporeal, yet ghostly; present, yet inaccessible'. Letters were 'tiny wings in the hands of the men'. Each one had its soul, its character, its voice, 'a woman's love on the page' can lift someone out of his misery.

So too can a glimpse of life outside: 'The silent *quai* under the tall, green poplars, the shimmering water where trees trembled in reflection among patches of sky, the path along the bank where a child was running: This peaceful vision of life, glimpsed suddenly through the window calmed him.'

Even the coming of spring, 'bittersweet season' that it is, is impossible not to feel:

In April, with the first buds on our stunted trees, the first clear skies, the first warm days, such a powerful call seemed to come from the very heart of life that we all felt we were emerging, our nerves raw, from some great lethargy. April quickened our failing energies. Three hundred wooden shoes beat more smartly against the pavement in our round; broken marionettes began to straighten up again; grey faces were uplifted ...

In the same way, a thought or memory coming unbidden might bring some comfort, but it could never last:

Some times, especially in the evening, a noise from the street may reach the prisoner in his cell. An automobile sounds its horn. The bell of a trolley car rings out in the distance. Instantaneously, the image of the illuminated streets and of that trolley car appears in your mind's eye. You see the conductor taking the steering bar into his wool-gloved hands. You see everything. You breathe in the smell of asphalt and gasoline. And then everything vanishes ... the calm grayness of time sooner or later resumes its usual hue.

Sooner or later, everyone went to see the doctor. If he was lucky, a man might get some extra bread or even medicine, but what made a difference to so many people, Serge said with some insight, was that this involved moments of contact with *other men*. It was *this* that made their ailments subside. Serge was not being judgmental here; he's not saying people are pretending to be ill, but showing a subtle appreciation of the true nature of the psychosomatic. If the only way we can get care is by being ill, we become ill.

The prison hospital, too, provided considerable respite; one was allowed to walk in the infirmary 'garden'. The term garden is used here, Serge says, in its 'most perfunctory sense'; the barren pond, the stunted trees, the cropped bushes - this could be the square, he said evocatively, in some mining village in the north, the men survivors of a gas explosion, 'After all, one form of suffocation is much like another.' But even there, one could walk up and down these paths at will, 'Divine freedom of the body! We meet, we talk; divine freedom of the soul!' Here, too, even the barest of the natural world provides comfort; here are the white quartz pebbles that the men look for in the gravel, 'so velvet, so soft to the touch, so white that they bring to mind many forgotten things'. And the trees are not abstract, but 'real, accessible trees, whose bark we love to touch and on which we love to watch the ants climbing'.

Serge was clear about what was involved in the struggle of those who chose to resist, as opposed to going under. In a chapter called, 'Drunken boat', taking its title from the poem by the young Rimbaud, Serge said, in almost unbearable prose, that it was:

> ... a voyage toward the unknown. The march will be long, so long that there is nothing by which to measure its duration, through a relentless night strewn with pitfalls. Falling along the way would be like sinking into a dark lake on a moonless night under a leaden sky in solitude: No cry would ever be heard. So be silent, then, whatever happens. The fleeting circles would barely break the surface of the still water, which would soon close without a ripple over the drowned man.

This silence is not the silence of submission, but neither is it a silence of pointless resistance, however understandable. Something else is called for, an acceptance that is, at the same time, a refusal, of the status of prisoner - 'I will be Number 6731... a robot programmed to obey', because one has no choice, but not to be confined by this - 'I will be myself - a free man'. The stakes in this struggle were high:

> A victory over jail is a great victory. At certain moments you feel astonishingly *free*. You sense that if this torture has not broken you, nothing will ever be able to break you ... And when a broad ray of sunlight inundates the barred window, when good news comes in from the outside, when you have succeeded in filling the dismal day with useful work, an inexpressible joy may ascend within you, like a hymn.

But he is stunned, when he had served his sentence in full, not to feel the great joy he had anticipated, 'at this dark threshold to life', a brilliant formulation, capturing all the contradictory feelings of the moment. He felt, instead, a sort of oppressive anxiety and, at the same time, a certain joy in a negative sense, 'like a fleeting light at the bottom of a well', that if he were not, after all, going to be freed, he would kill himself. At the same time, Serge had the insight that nothing could be more disappointing than the long-awaited fulfillment of a wish, because the reality itself was too concrete. One came to the realization that one had been living on exaltation which, once gone, left in its place 'a great void in which things appear only as they are, nothing more'.

For a time, a brief time, he experiences what we know now as institutionalization, that state of mind in which individuals have become so used to their confinement, whatever its nature, that they find it very difficult, or even impossible, to leave. And if they do succeed, it is what takes them, sooner or later, back inside, to what is familiar:

> I will be free in a few hours. Free. The enormous word is written in flaming letters before me ... I am about to enter the unreal ... I can no longer imagine what life is ... I begin to love this darkness ... where every stone is familiar to me ... a world that has become a deep unforgettable part of me ... My heart aches as a corner of the workshop and certain faces appear before me. I am leaving, they are staying. The Mill is eternal. That must be it; I feel the mark of jail too deeply within. They no longer brand your shoulder with a hot iron; it is an inner wound that will start to ache tomorrow.

But he struggles, resolving to overcome this, not to carry away with him any defeat. The Mill has not worn him down. He will leave it with his mind intact, stronger for having survived, tempered by thought. He has not lost the years taken from him.

The narrator has, like Serge, been in prison while a long, destructive and bitter war has been fought outside; the prison has been 'an unbelievable island, cut off from the movement of history'. Once outside, the first human figure he comes across is like a specter, shockingly evoked, a ghost in uniform who transforms into reality the unreal landscape, 'this landscape of the world between', which he will never see again: 'Our ringing footsteps fall in together. The first man I meet on the threshold of the world is a man of the trenches.'

* * *

Within a year or so, Serge was in prison once again. This time, after the failure of the syndicalist uprising in Barcelona when he was in France trying to get to Russia in the early throes of revolution, he found himself interned in a concentration camp, in a disused convent, in the west of the country. He would make use of this experience in his second novel, *Birth of our Power*, which was published in France in 1931. This prison was nothing like the one in *Men in Prison*; it was, relatively speaking, lightly guarded, barbed wire, a row of sentries, a low wall covered by fragments of broken bottles. Even so, no one had yet managed to get out of it. The prisoners were free to associate with one another, to read, to discuss things, to walk about within the camp confines, and no one had to work. And yet they were still prisoners.

This little world within the world is powerfully depicted by Serge. The camp, he said, might have been the main square of 'a bizarre village where there aren't any women'.

In this 'little piece of Europe', there were Greeks, Macedonians, Bulgarians, Chetniks, Serbs, Russians, Alsatians, Spaniards, Belgians and Romanians - 'thieves, marauders, phony foreign noblemen, probable spies, certain victims, unlucky people, vagabonds, second offenders, undesirables, Germanophiles, simple-minded people, rebels, revolutionaries'. And, as the powerful in Europe started to fear more and more the threat to their power posed by the communists, there are 'Jewish tailors and restaurant owners' who were 'guilty of having, elbows on the counter, maintained the integrity of the Bolsheviks'. (Serge himself was interned as a Bolshevik sympathizer.)

The camp was a reflection of the society in which it sat. It was even possible to get rich there, as one of the men, Maerts, 'the buccaneer', does. There were the decent and the corrupt, the highly intellectual and those who have lost their minds; some eat well while others, like Antoine, a traveler, driven from his roads by the war, lived on potato peelings, carrot leaves and even-gnawed bones found in the garbage every night. At night, one of the barracks becomes like 'an inn of olden times, in an old port haunted by pirates'.

What makes life tolerable is the existence of a community of like-minded people and the continued existence of the life of the mind: 'We formed a world apart within this city. It sufficed for one of us to call the others together with that magic word 'Comrades', and we would feel united, brothers without even needing to say it, sure of understanding each other even in our misunderstanding.'

In their dormitory, there were always people pouring over their 'endlessly annotated, commented, summarized texts'. There, revolutionary figures from the past like Saint-Just, Robespierre, Babeuf, Blanqui, Bakunin, were spoken of 'as if they had just come down to take a stroll under the trees.' Even those with 'no great sense of history', still had some great stories to tell, like Dmitri, the Russian sailor, who almost got his whole crew of an English steamer to mutiny, after throwing inedible soup in the face of the first mate, but ended up in chains instead. And in the late afternoon, a few people from each room would assemble to hear someone read from the newspapers. This is how they hear what is happening in Russia, in fragments, which are often inaccurate, as when they hear that Lenin has been assassinated. In fact, he survived. But this also serves to emphasize their isolation from everything that is going on in the world, and their impotence, and to instill a sense of futility, of time running out, while great things were being achieved elsewhere. And these feelings turn into rage. They think about an uprising, but know it would be futile. With some insight Serge remarked on how one of their fears was precisely that of being cowardly and they were therefore afraid of 'throwing ourselves into an adventure ... out of our own impotence'.

And there was the ever-present threat of death, which came 'without fanfare, simply, faceless, without terror'. The camp is decimated by an epidemic of typhus, but the political Russians do better than others. Even in this regard, their solidarity makes them stronger. The emergency fund they had set up, though meager, provides just about enough for the least fortunate 'to keep the flame of life glowing, if only as an ember'. And, they do not allow anyone to be moved to the infirmary, which has been nicknamed the Morgue, because that is where people go to die.

Once again, it was time which was taken from the inmates and time which they had to contend with. And unlike criminal prisoners who know when they will be released however far in the future, they had no idea at all when they might be freed, and, if so, what will then happen to them:

Long walks in the yard, to kill the time. Rare were those, in this forced leisure, who still knew the value of time, who read, who sketched, who studied, Equally rare the obstinate ones who refused to let themselves go ... We stayed alive. The days passed by. The weeks, the months, the seasons, the battles, the revolution, the war passed by. Life passed by.

When the armistice comes, 'it exploded above us, like a dazzling rocket, tracing a meteoric curve through the sky of our gray life'. Suddenly there is joy at the prospect of freedom, 'the end of the nightmare'. But this is only the beginning of the end of their captivity as they must wait for negotiations about an exchange of prisoners over which they have no control whatsoever. But, in the end, they leave.

* * *

It is a century since Victor Serge began his years in prison. It may seem incredible now, but there was a time, not so long ago, when many of us on the left believed in the abolition of prison, that prison might be done away with, for all but the most dangerous people. (*The Politics of Abolition* (1974) was the title of radical criminologist, Thomas Mathiesen's fine book about the prisoners' movement in Norway and his involvement in it.) We argued that sending people to prison was unjust and unfair, that it was counterproductive, and that it was a mark of a disciplinary state. Serge's writings were among those that inspired us.

Things could not have turned out more differently. Our societies have become more, not less, punitive; almost everywhere, prison populations are higher than they ever have been. The provision of prison and associated services has become very big business indeed, one of the few growth industries. Prisoners are no longer transported around the country in the prominent and threatening 'black marias' of old, but in anonymous vehicles, which might easily be delivering groceries. The concentration camp, which Serge must have been one of the first to describe, has become a central feature of life in many authoritarian regimes.

The physical conditions of prison may well have improved in some countries, the specific details may be different from Serge's time, but *Men in Prison* today is completely relevant to our modern understanding of the central nature of imprisonment. It is a genuine classic of prison writing that transcends its time. Rarely has the brutality, the pointlessness, the tedium, the dehumanization of prison, been so memorably depicted, but without bitterness or self-indulgence.

Modern jails, Serge concluded, 'are imperfectible, since they are perfect. There is nothing left but to destroy them.'

2

Yesterday we were nothing: the experience of revolution

On his release from prison in 1917, Victor Serge went to Barcelona to take part in the planned syndicalist uprising there. This failed, bloodily, and Serge lost many friends and comrades. He then traveled to Russia to join the revolution there, eventually reaching Petrograd in 1919. Despite his anarchist past and libertarian convictions, he had decided that he would join the Bolsheviks, but do so 'independently, without renouncing thought or critical sense'. Serge believed that the Bolsheviks were profoundly mistaken in many ways, in their centralizing leanings and bureaucratic tendencies, their intolerance of difference and their unquestioning belief in the state. But, for Serge, they still represented the best hope for the revolution. One had to be with them and among them if one were to counter them 'with freedom of the spirit and the spirit of freedom'. Serge was widely respected outside the Party and enjoyed good, if sometimes strained relations with the non-Bolshevik revolutionaries, such as the anarchists and the Mensheviks, and with the cultural intelligentsia. From the outset he was actively involved in the revolution, both as an organizer and as a soldier. (Serge took part in the battle of Pulkovo Heights in October 1919, which would prove decisive in the defense of the city and of the revolution itself.) It was these experiences of revolution that would be the subject of his next two novels, *Birth of our Power*, published in France in 1931, and *Conquered City*, published the following year.

With no strong narrative to engage the reader, *Birth of our Power* is, to my mind, the least successful of Serge's novels. Sometimes one feels his struggle to find a new form for what he is saying. Serge was trying to take the novel away from a central subject, to capture a process, and he isn't always successful. There are times, too, when it feels as though he has been swept up in his creative processes, but forgets about his readers. And that is a pity because there are always passages of great lyricism, and Serge's descriptions - of people, of environments - are often arresting. And no one described the values of solidarity and courage, or changes in political consciousness, as he did.

Here, for example, is Serge's description of the group his narrator found himself in:

> There were at least forty or fifty of us, coming from every corner of the world - comrades, that is to say, more than brothers by blood or law, brothers by a common bond of thought, habit, language, and mutual help. No profession was foreign to us. We came from every conceivable background. Among us, we knew practically every country in the world, beginning with the capitals of hard work and hunger, and with the prisons. There were among us those who no longer believed in anything but themselves. The majority were moved by ardent faith; some were rotten - but intelligent enough not to break the law of solidarity too openly. We could recognize each other by the way we pronounced certain words, and by the way we had of tossing the ringing coin of ideas into any conversation. Without any written law, we comrades owed each other (even the most recent newcomer) a meal, a place to sleep, a hide-out, the peseta that will save you in a dark hour, the *douro* (a hundred sous) when you're broke (but after that it's your own look out!). No organization held us together, but none has ever had as much real and authentic solidarity as our fraternity of fighters without leaders, without rules, and without ties.

And there is the portrait of Dario, the agitator; up at 6am, he has time for a coffee only while standing in the street, and then a day of leafleting, meetings, speaking, standing on a chair, at factories. But the most tiring hour is when he has to meet Portez the cement worker and argue his positions once again. When the narrator thinks of expressing his doubts, he knows Dario would laugh, 'You distrust intellectuals, especially those who have tasted the poison of Paris'.

Serge was also trying to capture the change in political consciousness of those who wish to make their own future. The shoe-shine stand operator, Sanche *el Tuerto* ('One-eye'), who 'usually sees men only from the knees down', is barely literate, struggles to read, but when he picks up the revolutionary paper *Soli*. 'A sort of smile twists his mouth. He wouldn't be able to repeat or to explain what he is reading, but a great contentment flows into the marrow of his bones.' And when he says, simply, 'No time' to 'a rich French shoe', he is doing something momentous and the customer goes away with the understanding that 'something is happening in the world'. Sanche's 'No time', both 'worries and enlightens him immeasurably', much more even than the day's news of a German sinking of a Brazilian boat and the bombing of London by Zeppelins. He knows, or at the very least senses, that something is afoot, something that he does not yet understand.

But the changing consciousness is not confined to individuals. It is something that affects the collective which is transformed by an increasing awareness of its own power, which surges through the city like 'new blood injected into the arteries of an old organism', unseen but vividly experienced by those in the know:

Workers stream out through the dazzling city toward their houses in the poor quarters, their steps lightened, shoulders thrown back with a new feeling of power. Their hands never tire of caressing the weapons' black steel. And waves of pride

27

flow from that steel into their muscular arms ... to those precincts of the brain where, by a mysterious chemistry, that essential life force we call the Will is distilled...

As elsewhere, Serge is particularly attuned here to people's subjective experience, what it *feels* like to be poor, to *feel* degraded, as the workers do, by 'the contrast between their sloppy old suits or overalls and bourgeois dress', when they pass expensive restaurants and luxurious cafes they never enter, or shop windows with astonishing displays of objects, 'so beyond their means as to be not even tempting'. It is here they 'encounter the women of that other race, sheathed in precious fabrics, their complexions colored by good health and luxury as if by a soft inner light ... the well-fed men with relaxed faces, haughty, superior looks, under broad felt hats'.

And he evokes powerfully the sheer physicality of being in a mass of people: 'Heads, bodies, hands are growing all around us like tropical vegetation; a powerful odor of warm and vibrant flesh - the smell of masses of men and of sunlight - makes our nostrils throb. I also breathe in the avid smell of the oranges being eaten greedily by a young girl ...'

Serge was also a keen observer of the places he found himself in and powerfully evoked these topographies, these physical contexts, as he does in this book, which opens with the words, 'This city and us'. And later on he remarks, 'Every city contains many cities. This was ours. We did not penetrate into the others.' Serge beautifully describes the landscape, the 'craggy mass of sheer rock - shattering the most beautiful of horizons', that towers over this city. It is 'crowned by an eccentric star' of jagged masonry cut centuries ago into the brown stone which now conceals secret constructions under the innocent grassy knolls. The secret citadel underneath lends 'an evil aspect' to the rock, which, between' the limpid blue of the sky, the deeper blue of the sea, the green meadows of Llobregat and the city, resembles a strange primordial gem'. We would have loved this rock, Serge says, had it not been for the way in which it had become an instrument of oppression, for the mountain was 'a prison - subjugating the city, blocking off its horizon with its dark mass under the most beautiful of suns'. The landscape, in other words, which might seem natural to most people, is itself political and saturated with history. It is a continual reminder of oppression, and even death:

> Our voices would suddenly drop off, when, at a bend in the path, the stark, grass-covered corner of the citadel's ramparts loomed up before us. The name of a man who had been shot was on all our lips. [Francisco Ferrer, libertarian educator, executed in 1909] We used to stop at certain places from which we could see the narrow confines of the dungeons. Somewhere within these fortifications, men like us, with whom each of us at one time or another identified ourselves, men whose names we no longer remembered, had undergone torture not long ago...

People's names and faces may have been forgotten with the passing of time, but what remains is 'a searing, confused feeling for the indignities suffered in the cause of justice'. The pain these men suffered comes to be remembered 'as one remembers something one has suffered oneself ... And, from that, I had an even greater sense of the communion between their lives and ours'.

And there is the constant awareness of the danger faced by those at the forefront of the struggle:

> And the idea I am trying to get rid of pierces me, like an electric needle, from one temple to the other: Dario will be killed, for that city, for us, for me, for the future. Every morning when he leaves the house where he has slept, every

evening when he enters the back rooms of little cafes where fifteen men - including one traitor - are waiting for him, at every moment of his patient agitator's labor, he moves toward that end marked out for him.

And even in the maelstrom of political upheaval there is room for love:

He pressed herself close to him without speaking a word. He sought her face and found only her ardent lips. "Let me look at you," he said. He struck a phosphorous match against the wall. A sputtering blue star, hissing and spidery, burst into flame at his fingertips, her delicate, soft-toned face - with its huge dark eyes, each now lighted by a spark, shining from out of their deep-set, dusky orbits - was nestled in the hollow of his arm, with a poor, gentle, worried smile. Dario gazed at it until the ephemeral light singeing his fingers went out. They made love in total darkness - in silence, for he was hurried and tired, and she always felt on the verge of losing him.

* * *

The uprising having failed, the narrator is on the run in Paris whose beauty 'smiles on implacably like summer'. It is a bad day, he says, and he runs all over Paris in search of refuge but his 'addresses are running out, and time is moving on'. He worries that the papers he has will not stop him being arrested if he is forced to register at a hotel. 'Where to find a roof tonight? A few hours under shelter, time to recharge my nervous equipment, and the future is saved.' He eventually ends up at a sixth-floor door in 'this enemy city' where he is told he is in luck, that the man's girlfriend walked out on him recently, leaving him more room. He reassures him wonderfully saying, 'You'll be all right here. I have an excellent reputation; you can sleep with both eyes shut.'

The man with the 'excellent reputation' is Broux, who despite 'his worn-out lungs, his obstinate self-effacement, his bookish timidity', is a strong man, strong by means of his 'awareness of how impossible it is to live, he raises himself precisely to a higher possibility of living, to an endurance which is more sure of itself because it believes it has nothing more to lose. From his weakness he was able to create a strength, from his despair, an acquiescence, from his acquiescence, a hope ...'

Outside, and almost as a backdrop, there is a war going on. Somewhere, up there above these clouds, 'men dressed in leather are trying to fix this city in their bombsights'. The anti-aircraft guns produce in response, 'explosive blossoms'. Serge remarks, without any irony, that civilization reaches its high point in this 'senseless combat' above the Louvre, as 'Masterpieces of ingenuity, summing up the work of all races in all times - millions of men suffering, striving, daring - seek each other out, with the greatest human lucidity, in order to destroy each other ...'

When they eventually reach the Russian border, there is no great welcome, only the 'indifferent expressions, undernourished looks' of the guards:

Never could the idea come to anyone to rush toward them with outstretched hand saying *Brothers!* for they belonged entirely to a world where words, feelings, fine sentiments shed their prestige immediately on contact with primordial realities. One could only have talked to them about a fire in front of which you could warm up, about shoes to be mended, about flannels to keep your empty stomach warm, about hot soup with which to fill it. I stared intently at these silent men, standing there in such great distress. I thanked them for teaching me about true fraternity, which is neither in sentiments or words, but in shared pain and shared bread. If I had no bread to share with them I must keep silent.

The novel ends with the narrator remembering a letter he had received from Spain just before the final journey, that he has not yet read. As old books burn in the fire, he recalls 'the city we had not been able to take, our hope, our will, our power, our real power since I was about to go to sleep in a conquered city where ... this moment, this shelter, this warmth which allow me to think of you [his former comrades].' He imagines Dario walking in at that moment, to 'shrug his invisible burden off his shoulders', when his eyes alight on one line, 'no different from all the others in the forest of symbols ... "they killed our Dario".'

* * *

If *Birth of Our Power* doesn't always work well as a novel, *Conquered City* which followed, must be *the* novel of the revolutionary experience. Again, there is no central story but a series of narratives, different perspectives. Serge's use of montage or jump-cuts can be disorienting, but he makes us *feel* we are in the unnamed city, Petrograd, at a crucial point for the city, and the revolution for which it stands. The novel takes place in 1919/20 at a time when revolutionary Russia was threatened by its enemies within, who were backed by the major powers from outside, Britain, the United States, France who were appalled, and profoundly threatened, by this radical challenge to the established order, their order. 1919 saw the creation of socialist republics in Hungary and Bavaria, a workers' uprising in Germany, a general strike in Barcelona, and a general strike in Glasgow which brought tanks on to the streets of the city: 'How they long for our death back there, for the death of this Republic ... which is still the greatest hope ... the work of those who have always been vanquished, always duped first and then massacred ...'. Only yesterday, someone says, 'we were nothing ... we counted only as statistics: labor force, emigration, death rate, crime rate, suicide rate.' This is what the revolution challenges.

The title, of course, is ironic, but sadly so. The city, as the novel shows clearly, is far from conquered: it reflects the growing awareness of one of the narrators who has arrived in the country with great expectations only to see a very different reality at almost every turn:

We have conquered everything and everything has slipped out of our grasp. We have conquered bread, and there is famine. We have declared peace in a war-weary world, and war has moved into every house. We have proclaimed the liberation of men, and we need prisons ... and we are the bringers of dictatorship. We have proclaimed fraternity, but it is the 'fraternity and death' in reality.

Even the snow is not bright, but grey. Everywhere there is a prehistoric gloom because there is no power. Everywhere people are hungry, everywhere the people are cold. They keep their old fur coats on and they rip up floorboards in old houses to keep their fires going. The factory chimneys no longer smoke unless there is some emergency work to be done. People work in semi-darkness because there is no power. There is typhus and the threat of cholera. And the spring thaw will, within a few days, make cesspools of the frozen piles of excrement in the court-yards. We feel the cold along with Professor Lytaev, who still teaches a class at the university in the evening as if 'in a city of another time, in the middle of an abandoned monastery'. He has to keep his fur cloak and hat on while his audience listen 'frozen, in their coats'. 'Hard rectangles of night pressed in through the white frost-ferns on the windows.' We experience the constant plotting and threats to the revolution from within: 'Everywhere the enemies of the revolution are active: The Counterrevolutionary Centre Right organization could count on

146 confederates in the city, organized in groups of five, and a thousand sure sympathizers. These forces could be mobilized in a single night.'[7] Chapter 11 starts, 'The 1st Estonian Regiment went over to the enemy on May 24. The 3rd Infantry of the Second Brigade turned traitor on May 28...'

The revolution is already over-reacting massively, 'spider webs knocked down with ax blows'. An anarchist bomb attack is used as a pretext to execute no fewer than sixty-seven people, 'spies, counterrevolutionaries, foreign agents' but also, 'ex-financiers, ex-high officers, monarchistic professors, vice-den operators, and unlucky adventurers'. The report of their deaths fills two tiny columns in the barely legible newspapers plastered on the walls. At a time when the southern front in the civil war was going badly, 'Sixty-seven? The price in blood of a skirmish ...'

And all the time, people's hearts and minds are being hardened. When a vote is taken at a Special Commission (Cheka) hearing, only one person, Kirk, dares to vote against the death sentence. The chair, Osipov, dismisses him saying they must be pitiless and share the responsibility. 'You're a Don Quixote', he tells Kirk, 'with your lone horsemen's ways ... this affair no longer has any importance. No more than your death or mine would have this week.' So too, Danil, who has nothing but contempt for intellectuals, who haven't 'the least idea of the stench of a sacked town or the look of an open belly full of fat green flies over which poppies droop their heads', dismisses historian Platon Nikolaevich's resort to Dostoyevsky. The Karamazovs, he says, 'split hairs with their beautiful souls; we are carving flesh itself and the beautiful soul doesn't mean a damn thing to us. What is serious is to eat, to sleep, to avoid being killed, and to kill well. There's the truth.'

A 'monstrous state' is arising, devouring its enemies, real and imagined, as happens to many of the people we encounter here. And at the same time, the new administration must also address the ordinary problems of everyday life in a city and Serge vividly

conveys the enormity of the tasks facing those who want to build
a new order:

> Other oases of electricity burning from dusk to dawn: the
> Committees, Committees of Three, of Five, of Seven, of Nine,
> the Permanent, Temporary, Special Subaltern, Superior,
> Supreme Committees deliberating on the problem of nails, on
> the manufacture of coffins, on the education of preschool
> children, on the slaughter of starving horses, on the struggle
> against scurvy, on the intrigues of the anarchists ... on road
> transport ... So much thought straining and working every-
> where in these messy rooms under the same portraits, in that
> same atmosphere of neglect characteristic of conquered
> places where people are always rushing in and out.

Serge is also alert to the new bureaucracy that is taking shape
and which is wonderfully captured in this passage, with its
echoes of the depictions of city life by other modernist writers,
notably TS Eliot and Virginia Woolf:

> Around ten o'clock the street took on a feeble animation.
> People suddenly rushed by on urgent, necessary, imperious,
> deadly tasks. They moved quickly, similar in their diversity -
> uniforms and black leather - men and women alike, young or
> ageless, carrying overstuffed briefcases under their arms:
> dossiers, decrees, transcripts, theses, orders, mandates,
> absurd plans, grandiose plans, senseless paperwork and the
> quintessence of will, intelligence, and passion, the precious
> first drafts of the future, all this traced in little Remington or
> Underwood characters, all this for the task, for the universe;
> plus two potato pancakes and a square of black bread for the
> man carrying these burdens. This was also the hour when
> those who had accomplished the tasks of the previous night
> returned homeward, chilly and agitated with oddly wrinkled

yellowed faces, yet feeling a final rush of energy mixed with their fatigue.

And all the time there is the stunning contrast between the grandeur of the city, built by the modernizing Peter the Great in the early years of the eighteenth century as his new capital, and the misery which now prevails. Grimy red flags hang from the eighteenth century Italianate palaces, 'Nobility and grandeur still showed through the rags and tatters'.

Laundry hangs from dirty windows on the main boulevard, while the chimney pipes of little iron stoves, spitting out their puffs of dirty black smoke, poke through broken windows:

Mud-spattered shop fronts, crumbling facades, shopwindows full of bullet-holes and held together with tape, splintered shutters, watchmakers' shopwindows displaying three watches, an old alarm clock, and one fancy pendulum; unspeakable grocery stores; herb teas packaged to look like real tea, as if there were still fools so stupid as to be taken in by these labels, tubes of saccharine, dubious vinegar, tooth powder - brush your teeth carefully, citizens, since you have nothing to use them on ...

In the countryside, source of the grain which the city needs if it is not to starve, murderous divisions are emerging all the time and families are divided against one another:

The harvest had been brought in the countryside. It was being hidden. Tillers who fought under the red flags with their old scythes buried the wheat and sounded the tocsin at the approach of the Anti-Christ. Others, their sons, with red stars sewn into their old Imperial Army caps, arrived to search their barns. Workers, fearful of being stoned, harangued village elders. They were men caught between hunger, hatred, discipline, faith, war, fraternity, typhus, and ignorance.

And in the chaos that prevails, the most ordinary, unexceptional individuals acquire an appalling power, 'a non-com transformed into an ataman had railroad workers thrown into locomotive boilers alive. But, a son of the people, he gave the daughters of his old generals to his exasperated soldiers ...'

At the same time, Serge is alert, as he always is, to the beauty and joy that are present despite the cold, the hunger, the fear: 'Scattered bursts of laughter hung in the woods among the slim white trunks of birches. Specks of dull silver seemed to hang in the air.' (This has echoes of those amazingly condensed poems of the imagists, such as Pound's poem about the Paris Metro.) And after Xenia, the young Party member, has carried out the searches assigned to her one night, she decides to go for a walk. She stops to look at a single white cloud, reflected in the water of the canal, floating 'in the sky of that water' as if above the city:

When we are dead, thought Xenia, when everything is finished, perhaps a similar cloud will pass through a similar sky at this very spot. What eyes will see it reflected in this water, eyes that will have known neither war, nor famine, nor fear, nor anguish, nor night patrols, that will not have seen man strike down man? I can't even imagine it.

And people still are in love, as are Olga and Arkadi:

She was happily aware of the red glow of his cigarette in the semidarkness. She loved to move about in the invisible light of eyes following her from the far end of a dimly-lighted room. Nowhere in the world could anyone give this man a greater feeling of calm, a more secure rest, a surer joy. She knew this. And the warmth of his eyes resting on her, soft at first, then imperious like a magnet, enveloped her wholly, imparted new suppleness to her movements. Somewhere deep inside, her whole being cried out that this was an immense happiness ... she laughed silently.

Although even this most private realm is not totally removed from the political context, as when Xenia worries if she should wear French perfume when she goes to meet Rhyzik, 'Was the use of these luxuries invented by the depravity of the rich not unworthy?... Wouldn't he be angry at this bit of refinement in her?'

* * *

If *Birth of our Power* is a novel about the unsuccessful bid for power, and *Conquered City* the struggle to hold onto power, part of Serge's last novel, *Unforgiving Years*, is about the revolution gone wrong. D, a long-time Communist, has decided while in Paris that he must, finally, break with the Party. Using the skills he learned as a Comintern agent, he is on the run from his former masters but he is taking so many precautions that he starts to wonder if by the very act of doing so, for example by changing taxis, he is drawing attention to himself. And, in any case, how easily he might have been seen, just by chance, by one of his numerous faceless pursuers. When he is hiding out in a small hotel, everything he hears or sees may be significant and dangerous - a time given for a taxi, or the time of arrival of a telegram may be codes. 'I'm going crazy', he thinks.

Here, Serge was using his own experience as an agent of the Communist International (Comintern), set up by the Bolsheviks in 1919 to promote revolution abroad. He worked with revolutionary organizations in Germany and Austria and reported to the International on the developing situation. (His published reports are collected in the volume, *Witness to the German Revolution*.). This was, at times, incredibly dangerous, and some pages of the *Memoirs* dealing with this period read like a thriller.

Foolishly, D has announced his resignation before escaping.

This is not formally a capital offense but only because it is simply unthinkable. An unwritten law, Serge writes, dictated the elimination of agents who disobeyed, and disapproval of the regime was the worst form of disobedience since it implied the use of the individual conscience whose existence could not even be brooked, for what it might do to the ruling edifice of iron discipline. The idea that anyone might bow out without betraying, or withdraw into a state of simple insignificance, any superior believing this would be thought a lunatic or an accomplice to be himself eliminated.

Even as he looks forward to his rendezvous with Nadine, he worries that she too is being caught up in an invisible net, precisely because she is to be trusted and because she is bound to him by 'a friendship more definitive than love'. The bare fact of her connection to him puts her in extreme danger.

And yet the ordinary life of the city goes on and is beautifully evoked: 'Morning purity of cobbles and asphalt ... a dappled light under which one would wish to live for a long time, meditating'. At the same time, there is the appalling complacency of the city in the face of its future, with its 'windows of clockmakers, cobblers, and booksellers, the elaborate food stuffs, the color postcards full of gross jokes and sexual innuendo ... in which human beings have attained the maximum possible degree of self-indulgence, and thus the height of freedom, of relaxation'. This city in which people are being hunted cannot see its own future which is so evident, 'A dangerous thing, relaxation ...'

3

Building on corpses: the repressive state

No one grasped the awful reality of repression in the Soviet Union more than Victor Serge did, and no one was better able to show the truth of what was happening than he did. Twenty years before Soviet leader Nikita Khrushchev would admit *some* of the truth of the Stalinist terror on 25 February 1956, in his speech to the 20th Party Congress, Serge was describing *in detail* what was going on in this country, a country he was the first to describe as totalitarian. (Although obviously of huge significance, equally important was the fact that Khrushchev's speech was itself given *in secret*. It was only published in full in Russia in 1989.) Serge's writings, such as *Destiny of a Revolution* and *From Lenin to Stalin*, also predate by more than 30 years Alexander Solzhenitsyn's monumental *The Gulag Archipelago*, a book that shocked the west with its horrendous account of the camps. (Solzhenitsyn says in his preface that, when he started to write the book in 1958, 'I knew of no memoirs or works of literature dealing with the camps'.)

Serge was the first person to describe in any detail the vast prison camp system in Russia. It was in 1937 that he wrote that the country had the largest concentration camp system in the world. There were forced-labor camps, dungeons, lumber camps, mines, even secret camps, camps notorious for their brutality or for their hunger, 'filthy corners from which there is no return'. There were camps, such as the SLON, the Solovietsky Special Camp, so vast they occupied 'an entire, vast northern country'. There were even model camps, 'attractive reform colonies for the edification of foreign investigators and movie-goers'. (Serge is here referring to a propaganda film made for foreign consumption.) The location of these, in the most remote and inhospitable areas, was not just to keep them away from the mass of the population. More important, the environment itself was a crucial feature of the punishment, killing many, but demoralizing and dividing those who managed to survive. Serge summed it up well:

> What cannot happen in a detachment of condemned men lost in the Siberian brush, including bandits, desperate or exasperated peasants, stool-pigeons ready for anything, intellectuals and technicians, harshly treated politicals, all of them bound to a hard task, badly fed, and submitted to the absolute power of a policeman who is himself a condemned man?

Serge also quoted from a brief newspaper report, the message of thanks sent to Stalin by miners in Karaganda to Stalin. Nowhere is it said that this mine is at the centre of a vast concentration camp, that the work is done by prisoners, that perhaps some of the signatories themselves are condemned men, that the Karaganda is 'one of the most dreaded camps for the hunger that reigns there, for its remoteness from all civilization, for the harshness of its inner rule'.

Serge also saw the crucial importance to the Soviet state of internal passports, probably unique in modern times, which served to control, not just the movement of ordinary people as the name suggests, but their everyday lives. Passports were always refused to families of people who were executed or sent to prison for long periods. So anyone without a passport was automatically suspect when looking for housing or work or, simply trying to buy anything, let alone in the eyes of the police. And the passport could always be marked at work to the serious detriment of the holder. Serge cites examples of workers who didn't turn up for days of 'voluntary labor', that is unpaid work to help meet targets, and who were sacked for 'sabotage of the production plan'. There was never any secret about the internal passport, yet it still came as a shock to many in the West to know these existed and what their effect was.

And, of course, Serge understood the complete power wielded by Stalin, a power that extended far beyond the borders of the country he ruled. Trotsky was, of course, killed by his agents thousands of miles away in Mexico, but he was only the most famous to be murdered on Stalin's orders. Andres Nin, Serge's friend and comrade from the POUM, was abducted on the streets of Barcelona and never seen again. In September 1937, Serge himself had been due to meet the NKVD agent, Ignace Reiss, who wanted to defect. He failed to keep the rendezvous arranged in Rheims and his bullet-ridden body was later found, with a ticket to Rheims in his pocket.[8]

* * *

After the 1917 revolution, the new government found itself in possession of the files of the Tsarist secret police, the Okhrana, and one of the many tasks Serge was entrusted with was to make a study of these. What he and his colleagues found provided an astonishing insight into the workings of a repressive regime. In a secret room in the Okhrana building in Petrograd, accessible only to the chief of police and the officer in charge of the files, they found dossiers on more than 35,000 provocateurs. These Tsarist agents included a man who had been the exiled Lenin's spokesman in the Russian parliament, Malinowsky, and also the head of the Social Revolutionary party's terrorist organization, at a time when it was engaged in carrying out assassinations. (When a Commission was established after the revolution to question former police officials, it turned out that two members were themselves former Tsarist agents.)

Serge also discovered a series of files on himself, even though he had returned to Russia only in 1919, after the fall of the Tsar. The Okhrana clearly had paid great attention to the activities of revolutionaries abroad; when the Russian embassy in Paris was handed over to the Provisional Government, files there showed that 15 Tsarist agents had been working in that city alone and, what's more, that a prominent French journalist, head of the foreign desk at the leading paper, *Le Figaro*, was also on the Okhrana payroll.

The files made Serge think about the psychology of the provocateur or informer, what it was that made people betray their supposed comrades and friends. Serge used as an example a woman, Serova, who had informed on revolutionary groups, betraying the location of literature and weapons, as well as individuals, who were then arrested. She was, Serge said, 'a weak character, living in poverty, who works courageously as a party member'. She is arrested. 'Abruptly torn out of her normal existence, she feels lost.' Fearing forced labor or even death, she realizes that she can avoid this fate if she says 'a word, just one word', about someone who actually had done her some wrong. She hesitates. But 'an instant of cowardice is enough; and there is plenty of cowardice in the depths of a human being. The most terrible thing is that from now on, she will no longer be able to turn back ... They have her now.'

Far more dangerous for Serge, however, were those who were not cowards, but who believed in nothing and who cared nothing for the cause they served, taken by the idea of danger, intrigue, conspiracy, 'a complicated game in which they can make fools of everyone'.

In the files, Serge also found what he described as among 'the saddest of human documents'. - receipts for payments involved in the execution of political opponents; the cost of setting up a gallows, the travel, return, of a priest. and, of course, the hangman's traveling expenses.[9]

* * *

Midnight in the Century, written by Serge while himself in exile, is the story of a group of oppositionists, in internal exile in the fictional place, Chernoe. A central part of the story is how they are ensnared in the murderous machinations of the leader. The novel begins with the lecturer, Mikhail Kostrov, having an uneasy feeling that something is about to happen to him. He is arrested in the street and thrown for several weeks into, what Serge calls, 'Chaos', in a hideously over-crowded prison, cut off from the world with no information about the charges against him. ('If the houses of detention are overcrowded', a judge tells him, 'it is not the fault of the proletarian dictatorship but that of the counter-revolution which assails us on every side'.) One day, he gets a parcel from his wife of boiled eggs and, even though it has been broken open by the guards with a dirty knife, he is relieved because he understands the messages implicit in the package; he knows this would not be allowed in serious cases. It also means his wife is still working.

After several months detention he is finally questioned and it quickly becomes clear that he has been watched closely. He is confronted with statements he has made in lectures and articles he has written which are taken to be critical of the regime. When he refers to disorders in Uzbekistan he is warned of 'domestic espionage', and even the 'scornful way' he pronounced certain names in private is evidence of his oppositional tendencies. Kostrov is also confronted with a joke against the leader that he has told. About the actress to whom he shared this joke, he is told, 'You sent her far, to a very cold climate'. (Elsewhere, Serge relates the true story of how a seemingly private joke can have the most appalling consequences. Two couples who are out for a drive and are slightly drunk. They get a puncture and one of them makes a joke about an explosion under Stalin's behind. Several months later, the two women fall out and the remark is reported; the man who made the joke gets ten years in prison for terroristic agitation, and the two women five years for failing to report it.)

The next day, Kostrov decides to give in, 'and wrote out one more surrender' with 'all the right words ... the edification of socialism, the great wisdom of the CC [Central committee], the correctness of its tactics, the repudiation of errors due to lack of understanding, to the petty bourgeois spirit, to the counter-revolutionary influence of comrades now denounced and capitulated'. When he finishes he hears himself say, 'Go on, you rotten fraud.'

The fourth part of the book, 'Directive', is a chilling account of a meeting of the Politburo. Stalin is thinking about how to use the forthcoming party conference to his best advantage. He needs to install 30 new regional secretaries, involving 30 dismissals in disgrace, which threaten 300 influential local secretaries, 3000 less influential local secretaries, 30,000 even less influential local secretaries - none of which will be discussed. The dismissals are necessary to get rid of people who implemented a plan that resulted in two failed harvests. That the plan was his is fatally beside the point.

Serge shows how the directive will have to be carefully worded for maximum political effect, to take account of all the convolutions of the leader's mind; it must be both very obscure and very precise at the same time; it must foresee eventualities, even if these are contradictory; it must command definite actions, while suggesting various others so as to permit effective repudiation of anyone who might carry them out. Those around Stalin understand that the greatest danger was not the visible one, it is the one 'which cannot be unmasked because it does not yet exist in the facts: analysis reveals it lying latent among the masses'. One man's paranoia had become a whole system of thought.

In charge of the Chernoe exiles is GPU officer Fedossenko.[10] When he receives the directive, it is immediately clear to him what he must do, prepare a case against several of them and, even as he reads the order, 'faces appeared clearly before his eyes, faded, re-appeared ... Ryzhik, Elkin, Varvara ... Tabidze, Avelii ... Kostrov'. Fedossenko 'was satisfied with himself'. In fact, his unfailing intuition had already in effect anticipated the directive. He already has a hold over Varvara, who was sacked over a stolen loaf (it was stolen by the delivery man; Kostrov is implicated in the alleged sabotage of a consignment of school notebooks, (they have a simple misprint in a table), and is suspected of 'duplicity toward the central committee' (Fedossenko has a copy of his statement of repentance). Moreover, a woman with whom Kostrov has become friendly, Maria Ismailova, is an informer.

At first, Fedossenko tries a friendly approach to Kostrov, 'I'm talking to you as a comrade', telling him he is sure the Party will re-admit him soon. But Fedossenko is up against time, he needs to get his report done in time for it to be useful in the preparations for the party conference. He is also ambitious and wants very much to see his report published in the monthly bulletin of the Security Department. But even Kostrov is resisting, despite the lack of news from his wife and child, the filthy cell he is kept in, and the fact that every day he looks older. Meanwhile, Rodion says he will confess, 'For everything. I'm the one who did everything. Alone, I confess!' This, of course, is completely useless as there has to be a conspiracy.

In the end, Fedossenko himself is accused of incompetence, of chasing after minor crimes, while a 'secret Committee of Five' was carrying out its activities. A loose association of comrades has become the 'counter-revolutionary Trotskyite centre of Chernoe'. He is also accused of allowing the most dangerous Trotskyist to escape; in truth, Rodion, who managed to get away, is the least political of the group. He has also failed to inform Moscow of the 'active and organized counter-revolutionary Right opportunists in the distribution service of the Public Education Department right in Moscow'. He is relieved of his command, his physical being shrinks before his colleagues and, like a 'puppet or ghost', the 'demolished Fedossenko' is locked in a cell. (Serge was good at showing the rivalries among state officials, in this case how visibly relieved everyone is at the meeting when the blame is being pinned on Fedossenko, 'Six pairs of lungs exhaled the same *ouf* and the same thoughts of 'pig-face', big-shot'.)

Serge was also acute about the character types that inhabit the state machine, like the head of security, 'a middling-minded man', who sits slightly back from the table as a sort of self-effacement and whose cropped moustache reminded one that 'he shaved every morning, like an ordinary man, that he probably desired a woman, that he too lived an ordinary life'. And, at the same time, he is all too aware of his great importance, 'the eye and hand of the Party - The hand that searches. The hand that holds the handcuffs. The hand that holds the poison. The hand that holds the revolver in the service of the Revolution'. And if he didn't say this, his whole manner expressed it, 'shadow of the great men over whom he watches day and night, formidable shadow over the subordinates he commands in the name of danger and of safety, deadly shadow over the captives he sends to their fate in the name of a magnificent future'.

Of the accused exiles, only Rodion manages to escape although he nearly drowns in a river and is saved by a wild man, living completely outside society. He eventually gets to a town where he gets a job on a building site, in the 'Socialist Emulation' brigade. He is befriended by a woman who shows him how to carry the most number of bricks, in the most secure way, 'There was no time to breathe, to exchange a few words, or to smoke'. He discovers that they are building a new district HQ for state security.

* * *

Several years after *Midnight in the Century*, in *The Case of Comrade*

Tulayev, Serge took the political novel to a new level; compelling, deeply disturbing, above all, sophisticated in its understanding of the political maneuvering of a ruthless dictator who rules, not just by fear, but with the acquiescence or collusion of those around him and his subjects. Tulayev, a leading official, is being dropped off one night at his mistress's flat, when an office worker, Kostia, walking home, sees the official car of a man who is obviously important. He hears his driver say, 'Good night Comrade Tulayev' and immediately realizes who he is, the man responsible for the purges in the universities and for mass deportations. He takes out the gun he has just been given (slightly improbably, it might be said) and shoots him, 'The explosion was deafening and brief'. Kostia carries on home through the snow. We do not hear about him again until the end of the book.

Suspicion immediately falls on Tulayev's driver, who is brutally questioned and tortured. The account of this is particularly harrowing. The fact that he has been a good and trusted employee, is not only no help to him, but itself becomes a cause of suspicion when it is discovered that there are testimonials in his file from Nikolai Bukharin, whose driver he once was. Once a leading Bolshevik, Bukharin now stands convicted as a traitor and shot.

The case is being investigated by Erchov who, before his appointment, had thought himself 'happily forgotten' by the Personnel Service. In a particularly chilling scene, he is appointed by The Chief himself, amid a sea of smiling faces in the Kremlin. 'A heavy responsibility, Comrade Erchov.' he says, 'Bear it well.' It is as if Erchov knows, just as we imagine, his likely fate. Erchov had reached 'the pinnacle of his life', but is now afraid, now he faces three thousand dossiers all calling for the death penalty, 'three thousand nests of hissing vipers'. Erchov comes under increasing pressure to investigate Rublev, a former leading Bolshevik, associate of Bukharin and others now dead, but he knows there is nothing to link him to the case, 'not a shadow of a connection'. What there is rather is a trap for him, Erchov.

Eventually, Erchov is ordered to take a rest. Chillingly, his superior quotes Goethe to him, 'Kennst du das Land wo die Zitronen bluhn?' ('Do you know the land where the lemon trees blossom?') And he and his wife, Valia, travel on a special train to a resort reserved for party officials. When the train stops at a deserted station, he is summoned to take an important phone call, but is instead shown the order for his own arrest and stripped of his uniform and his authority. He has become such a professional that he even finds himself thinking that whoever organized this has to be complimented. The train, meantime, goes on with his wife. Assurances to him about her future serve only to underline her certain fate.

The murder investigation also implicates Makeyev, a peasant who has risen in the ranks of the Party and who was known as an enemy of Tulayev. A true mediocrity, brilliantly described, he had 'learned the official phrases which bring peace to the soul' and was 'exceptionally gifted in the art of forgetting in order to grow greater'. Of the little peasant he once he was, he 'preserved only a rudimentary memory, just enough to make him proud of his transformation'. Violent to his wife, he has nevertheless managed to secure a good post for his mistress. He boasts at one point, 'Men like myself have to have hearts of stone. We build on corpses, but we build'.

Serge brilliantly describes how the investigation almost takes on a life of its own:

> The case ramified in every direction, linked itself to hundreds of others, mingled with them disappeared in them, re-emerged like a dangerous little blue flame from under fire-blackened ruins. The examiners herded along a motley crowd of prisoners, all exhausted, all desperate, all despairing, all innocent in the old legal meaning of the word, all suspect and guilty in many ways; but it was in vain that the examiners

herded them along, the examiners always ended up in some fantastic impasse.

Former investigator Erchov, meanwhile, has himself become one of the main suspects, and is being held in a timeless hell. He doesn't know whether it has been four weeks or five or six since his arrest and, anyway, what did normal time have to do with 'the fermentation of a brain between the concrete walls of a secret prison in the age of the rebuilding of the world'. (Serge himself once spent 85 days, nearly 3 months, in an inner GPU prison without reading or occupation of any sort, 70 of those were spent in total solitude, 'without even taking the air in the grey courtyard reserved for the more tractable prisoners'.) When he is eventually interrogated, he claims the allegations are 'absolutely insane ... sheer madness'. And yet, when The Chief himself questions him, he says 'exactly what Erchov would have said in his place, what Erchov, in his despair, ought to be thinking'. His voice is so like Erchov's own inner voice that 'it restored Erchov to complete lucidity, and even to a sort of assurance'. The Chief asks him for 'The objective truth ...'

With considerable insight, another prisoner tells Erchov that the Party cannot possibly admit that it is 'impotent before a revolver shot fired from no one knows where, perhaps from the depths of the people's soul...' and that The Chief is fully aware that a shot fired at Tulayev is aimed also at him. He tells Erchov he should simply confess. For his part, Makeyev does confess: 'He was loyal, body and soul. Adaptable too and he knew the Central Committee was always right, the Political Bureau always right, The Chief always right - the errors of power compel recognition, become Truth'. But when he signs his statement saying he wishes to confess and cease all resistance to the Party, only the M of his name 'was still strong, the other letters looked crushed'.

The case becomes the case of Makeyev, Rublev and Erchov. An attempt is made to implicate a fourth man, Ryzhik, an old

Trotskyist who is living completely alone but still under intense surveillance in a hamlet of five houses called Dirty Hole, 'at the junction of two icy rivers lost in solitude'. (When writing letters he uses the address, 'the Brink of Nothing'.) Ryzhik would normally have been an immediate suspect because of his 'moral solidarity with the guilty', but he is added to the case only for tactical purposes, those of public presentation, 'to make the case more convincing to foreigners', while the prosecution even discuss allowing him to protest his innocence. Ryzhik, however, refuses even to take part in the interrogation and decides to die by hunger strike. News of his dying causes great panic, 'I order him saved!' The Chief says, as though his will must prevail whatever the reality.

It is because of his political understanding and experience that Ryzhik is able to decipher 'the hieroglyphics ... branded ... into the very flesh of the country', in other words, to understand the real meaning of what is happening. But this ability to make sense of all the trials, and the endlessly elaborate conspiracies and machinations they claimed to expose, is also a terrible burden, leaving him with an agonizing feeling of vertigo. Moreover, what he sees is not just the machinations of power but the people behind it all, '... each hieroglyphic was human: a name, a human face with changing expressions, a voice, a portion of living history'.

When it becomes clear that The Chief wants a trial that will link Tulayev's killers to the Trotskyists in Spain, attention turns to Kondratiev, a Communist who has returned from Spain and who embodies the last of the genuine revolutionary spirit. Kondratiev has spent years doing the unglamorous work of organizing river transport; 'at a time when abandoned barges rotted along the banks, he harangued crafty and discouraged fisherman in forgotten settlements, got together teams of young men, appointed captains seventeen years old ... created a School of River Navigation ...'

Serge chillingly describes how Kondratiev's colleagues at work at the Combustible Trust start behaving just slightly oddly to him once word gets around that he has fallen under suspicion in some way. He himself has no inkling. His secretary comes into his office 'too silently', her mute lips outlined in 'too harsh a red', her eyes looked frightened and she does not use the word 'comrade'. Others avoid him; a man, once a protégé, leaves by a back entrance after a lecture in order not to have to speak with him, a colleague shakes his hand in such a strange fashion that Kondratiev rubs his hands to get rid of the feeling, and he does not offer him a lift as he usually does. Only the young female students who genuinely know nothing sit with him. (In the end, Kondratiev is temporarily reprieved with a post in gold production in Siberia.)

Xenia Popov, who is in Paris on Party business, hears about the case and tries desperately to save Rublev's life. 'Grace, grace for Kiril Rublev, grace', she wants to telegraph, but to whom? Only The Chief can possibly save him and he will not get the letter in time, even if he reads it. She sends a message to her father, asking him to intervene, and she calls on Professor Passereau, 'famous in two hemispheres', President of the Congress for the Defence of Culture, and a member of the Moscow Academy of Sciences, asking that he send a message of support for Rublev. While claiming to be more moved than he can express, Passereau proceeds to give every reason he can for doing nothing - that he respects Russian justice, that he met Rublev only once, that his committee meets only once a month, that he has little influence, that they have other cases to pursue, and so on.

Xenia is also warned off her activities by a senior embassy official, who accosts her in a cafe, reminding her that what she is doing will have consequences for her father who is still in Russia. She is tricked into returning home, where she is of course arrested, while her parents are put under house arrest and their phone disconnected, their contact with the outside world cut off.

A friend, Gordeyev, warns him of the seriousness of possible charges, attempted desertion during a mission, 'activities contrary to the interests of the Union' 'Shivering into himself, Popov became so old that he lost all substance'.

Meanwhile Kostia, Tulayev's actual assassin, is living in the 'Road to the Future' kolkhoz, in love with his girlfriend, Maria, and struggling to meet the production targets set by the Plan. It is only when he comes to see his friend, Romachkin, from whom he obtained the gun, and happens to see the newspaper with its brief item about the confession of three men for espionage, treason and murder and their execution, that he learns the consequences of his action. Romachkin tells him it is too early for justice, 'What we have to do is work, believe in the Party, feel pity. Since we cannot be just, we must feel pity for men ...' Romachkin had learned of the case at a party meeting and, after an initial moment of hesitation, had raised his hand in support of the verdict and sentence, along with everyone else.

Kostia feels utterly alone. There is no one he can talk to about this. Maria does not want to know and, when she senses the true meaning of what he is saying, tells him, 'I know how much harm is done when the struggle is desperate ... there is a great and pure force in you ...'. In utter desperation, he writes an anonymous letter of confession. Comrade Fleischman, who is sorting out the files, 'thousands of pages, gathered into several volumes', reads it and, sensing the truth of what it says, finds himself close to tears. He lights the candle used for sealing letters, which is stained with red, and 'In the flame of the bloodstained candle' he burns it and crushes the ash in his hands. He drinks some tea and, 'Half aloud, with as much relief as gloomy sarcasm' announces, 'The Tulayev case is closed.'

Serge based his novel on the actual assassination of Sergei Kirov, a party functionary in Leningrad in December 1934. The assassin was a party member, Leonid Nikolayev, who would be tried in secret and shot before the end of the year. But Stalin used the murder for a brutal suppression of the opposition, described by Serge in a particularly harrowing chapter in *Destiny of a Revolution*, his detailed account of the state of the country 20 years on. He tells us that 114 prisoners, imprisoned before the shooting on terrorism charges, mostly people who had simply entered the country illegally, were summarily shot after the retroactive application of a decree speeding up executions after sentence. Later that month, 15 former leaders of the Leningrad Opposition were arrested, including Zinoviev and Kamenev, both old Bolsheviks and even associates of Stalin. As they could not be clearly linked to the murder, they were sentenced to long periods in prison for having formed a tendency in the Party. There were also mass deportations from all the major cities. Serge quotes a French technician living in Leningrad who estimated the number at 'close to one hundred thousand … The railway stations were bottled up for two weeks … The unfortunates sold their personal property on the railway platforms and eight days later the State stores could be seen chock-full of second-hand furniture'. As to those deported, this technician who knew several described them as 'very honest collaborators in Soviet technique and science'.

The novel is a terrifying account of how a state can exercise power over individuals leaving them helpless, using the threat of reprisals against their loved ones: Xenia acts according to her conscience, but in so doing she puts her father and mother at grave risk. And how, seemingly effortlessly, it can weave a web of accusations to suit whatever purpose it has in mind. Also how personally terrifying the leader had become; Kondratiev's secretary takes a call from him in 'terrified reverence', and Erchov, as we saw, has internalized him so much he has lost his own identity. And also how the state implicates thousands of ordinary citizens in its behavior in seeking public demonstrations of support for its actions and, in the process, eliminates the individual conscience.[11]

4

A stranger to no land: the experience of exile

Serge spent many years of his life in some form of exile, first in Orenburg, near Kazakhstan, 1,000 miles from the Soviet capital, then in Europe and, finally, in Mexico. Not only was he able to understand what this actually meant as a human experience; he was able to capture it in his writing in ways that no one else had done. In *Midnight in the Century* (1939) and in *The Long Dusk* (1946), both written in exile, and his poetry, most of which was written in Orenburg, he brought to life the endless fear, uncertainty, loneliness and poverty of exile, but also the incredible solidarity, and love, that was found there.[12]

Although those in internal exile had a freedom those in prison did not, the conditions of their lives were generally appalling. They were forced to live in remote, inhospitable places, and were usually ostracized by the local communities. They were expected to survive on even less than the already minimal rations. And they were subject to endless surveillance by the various authorities, and severely restricted in their movements. Their relatives were also subject to constant harassment.

As mentioned in the last section, *Midnight in the Century* is the story of five oppositionists in internal exile, their struggles to survive, to keep alive a belief in the possibility of the better kind of world they hoped they were building, and whose exile offers them no protection against forces larger than themselves. The miserable livelihoods which are permitted them are always at the mercy of a minor official's whim. Rodion, who has been working collecting rubbish, is sacked suddenly for no reason. His boss tells him, 'It's not my fault, you understand. I have an order.' This prompts Ryzhik's sardonic observation, 'The

Salvageable Rubbish Co-op no longer needs to draw up plans', and he asks if the rubbish is now escaping or if they are simply drowning in it. He is forced to rent just a corner of a room, with a mattress on it. Varvara is blamed for the disappearance of a loaf of bread and is also sacked. (In fact, it was taken by a delivery man.) And when a long-awaited consignment of school notebooks arrive and are found to have a misprint in a multiplication table, Kostrov, who is working in the local education department, is accused of sabotage. Even to take wood out of the river was a serious crime, as it belonged to the State Forest Trust and taking it, as Kurochkin did for firewood, meant 'risking jail or perhaps worse'.

Even doing something as ordinary as buying cigarettes, when a long-awaited consignment arrives at the town, becomes an occasion for them to be harassed and discriminated against. 'They're workers' cigarettes,' they're told, 'The counter-revolution has no right to them.' Others in the shop are glad, as it means there are fewer people to be served and more cigarettes to go round. Elkin is not bothered. 'We'll buy them in the private sector', he quips, 'there are some right here'. (Elkin is mocking Lenin's New Economic Policy, NEP, which allowed a limited form of private enterprise in the economy. and which many believed was a retrograde step.) The 'private sector' in this case is, in fact, 'the hands of a ragged, sunbrowned curly-headed urchin of under twelve'. 'The future of our country', Elkin remarks sardonically. (Elkin works in the State Fishery Trust working on plans for catches, storages and distribution. 'I know how many fish are supposed to be caught in five years,' he says at one point, 'Alas, nobody knows how many will be caught.')

The exiles decide to stop for a while in the sunlight which streams down on them, on the town, on the food queues and the fuel queues, and on 'the grey newspapers pasted on the wall to proclaim the triumphs of industrialization'. Elkin says, 'One day you'll lie down on a cot in a disheartening darkness. Then remember the sunshine of this moment. The greatest joy on earth, love apart, is sunshine in your veins.'

And, there is an ever-present fear of the larger forces against which exile is no defense and which can devour them at any moment. Ryzhik says at one point, 'Listen, brother, I'm uneasy. There are five of us - and not one informer! Do you think that's possible? And if it's like that, what do you think they're preparing for us, those bastards, with their thirty-six thousand dossiers?' What is being prepared for them becomes appallingly clear as the novel progresses.

As well as being about the terrible conditions of internal exile, this is very much a novel about solidarity. It is this that makes it a book of hope, as well as of tragedy. This solidarity is a bond among the exiles, but also a bond with other exiles and prisoners elsewhere. At one point in the story, Varvara receives a parcel. In it are food, cigarettes and a picture of her daughter, Katia, and also some books, including a copy of *The Arabian Nights*. The package has obviously been unwrapped, then redone by the secret police. Varvara and her friends are sure there is a message contained in it, but they cannot find it. Just as they are about to give up looking, something makes them cut open the back cover of the book: 'From the torn linen emerged, folded lengthwise, the thin slips which Ivanov had covered with microscopic callig-raphy in Projects Office No.4 of the SPCC. Special Purpose Concentration Camp, on Kola Peninsula. Avelii could not have felt more joy watching his trained falcon swoop down on a hare in the sweet-smelling grass.' The color drains from Varvara's face, as she looks at these letters, 'words, thoughts, truths for the Revolution. The meaning of our lives, since nothing else is left'.

And even in these awful conditions it is still possible for people to love one another; the novel contains one of Serge's most touching depictions of a relationship between a man and a woman in these times:

'Don't bruise me', is all Varvara can think to say to Avelii, 'seeking a tender word for him but not finding one ... They didn't go to sleep until they had talked for hours about so many things that it later seemed to them that they had tried to empty their lives in order to mingle them. They would never remember everything. These words exchanged, breath to breath, bodies entwined, hands seeking hands, would always yield new aspects, poignant and revealing. Like clouds scattered by a strong wind into momentary and never-quite graspable shapes.

The next day, Kostrov takes Varvara's arm in the street. He does so, saying 'How nice it is, Varvara Platonova,' when what he really feels is, 'a kind of gratefulness, as if he had said to her: I thank you for having those bright eyes, this slender neck, for carrying I don't know what joy within you.'

It is this sense of not being alone, of being part of something bigger than them, which gives them hope and makes it possible for them to live in this darkest hour, at midnight. In the same way, Elkin is elated when he was being transferred, to be allowed by his guard, 'a rather decent bugger', to go and look at an old stall selling all sorts of bits and pieces. There he finds an old copy of a book by Trotsky, the author's name scraped off the cover, 'They turned the first pages together smiling.' And when Rodion escapes and reaches the house of Galia, although she is disappointed that he is *not* Elkin, as she first imagines when she sees a figure in the bushes, she gives him everything she has, bread, onions, dried fish, a green apple, matches, some money, 'She filled his pockets, happy to touch him'. For his part, he felt 'overwhelmed by a happiness he did not yet deserve ...'

And once again we see that active acceptance of a given situation that is so often a feature of Serge's characters. When they are sitting in the sun with their cigarettes bought in the private sector, Rodion asks Elkin about the place of thought in these terrible times. Elkin replies that, 'it's something of a midnight sun piercing the skull' and wonders aloud, 'What's to be done if it's midnight in the century?' Rodion replies, 'Midnight's where we have to live then.' and, as he says it, he feels 'an odd elation.' To embrace reality, however awful, can bring a feeling of freedom.

Solidarity, for Serge, was not some romanticized, idealistic notion. It was very much a reality and something that he experienced, again and again, throughout his life. Recalling some of the people he met while in exile in Orenburg, most of them probably dead, he says, 'I am grateful to them for having existed, and because they incarnated an epoch'. He and his family had been able to leave the Soviet Union because of the campaign waged on their behalf by friends and supporters. A 'miracle of solidarity', Serge himself described it, but he was only too aware that others had not been so fortunate and would not be: 'It is humiliating to think that a certain sort of literary solidarity worked in my favor which won't work for others, simple and great revolutionaries without inkwells...No writers' congresses are likely to want to know about them'. And, of course, Serge used his freedom to work in solidarity, on behalf of those left behind, trying to tell people the truth about what was really happening there. He campaigned against the trials, setting up an international committee of enquiry whose members included the surrealist Andre Breton, the writer and militant Magdeleine Paz, and many others. (Serge insisted on the long title of 'Committee for Inquiry into the Moscow Trials and the Defense of Free Opinion in the Revolution' on the grounds that the revolution was not confined to the Soviet Union nor was Stalin's repression limited to there.)

And, later, in Marseilles and sliding, despite himself, into a state of despair as he waited for a place of refuge which he thought might never materialize, letters from the writer and editor, Dwight Macdonald, in New York, and from the poet, J-P Sansom, in Switzerland, 'seem to clasp my hands in the dark' and give hope. These were two men that Serge never met. And Serge and his family were able to escape from Europe because of these and many other people who sent him money, gave him work, and worked to get him papers.

* * *

It was while he was in internal exile in Orenburg, near Kazakhstan, that Serge wrote most of his poetry. The manuscript was one of the things stolen from him as he left the Soviet Union and he had to recompose the poems from memory.[13] They were published as a volume, *Resistance* in 1938, with an English translation by James Brook in 1972. In his introduction to the English edition, Richard Greeman finds echoes of many of the most interesting French modernist poets including Mallarme, Rimbaud, Appollinaire and Verlaine, along with many Russian writers with whose work he was well-acquainted. Serge was, he says, 'receptive to every mode of poetic intervention'. He was also, as we shall see in the next chapter, an insightful reader of his Russian contemporaries. Serge had loved poetry since he was a young man. It struck him, he said in his *Memoirs*, as 'a substitute for prayer ... so greatly did it uplift us and answer our constant need for exaltation'. The young Serge particularly loved the work of Paul Verhaeren, a precursor of Walt Whitman, for his 'anguished thoughts' on modern life. In his own poetry we see the same forces and values at work as in his other writings.

Like his fictional exiles, Serge in exile was still able to appreciate the natural wonder of the place he found himself in, despite the poverty and harshness of daily existence:

Vast, vast horizons, pure, distant, and light
soft grass, under the hot shimmering air,
vast, vast sky, forgotten blinding sky, impossible to look at.

('On the Ural river')

And watching a group of girls crossing the river, laughing and shrieking, he is moved by their delight, although he has to accept that it is, in the end, a simple one:

> What party, what love, what desire, what pleasure are they talking
> about to have that tinkling bell-like laughter?
> Probably none, they're laughing just
> because it's a nice day...

And he is too much of a realist to be caught up in any fantasy:

> I know that they will not have their promised joy,
> happiness is not on the other side of the river,
> the other face of the world will stay closed to them...

Nevertheless he carries this vision with him:

> They are on the other shore, four real girls,
> from my village of exile
> and their image has not failed in me. ('Four girls')

Exile was also a place for remembering, in particular, comrades from the past who are no longer alive, like Andre in Riga and Dario in Spain:

> O rain of stars in the darkness
> constellation of dead brothers!
> I owe you my blackest silence ... ('Constellation of dead brothers')

And he recalls, in two particularly telling lines, the personal sacrifices revolutionaries like him have had to make, unable even to live their own lives:

> We have never been what we are,
> the faces of our lives are not our own ... ('Confessions' section of 'History of Russia')

It was while he was in exile that he learned of the death of his friend, the Romanian writer, Panait Istrati. It was Istrati who had written the original preface to *Men in Prison* and who had published under his own name a book by Serge. Istrati had returned to Romania where he died from TB. Serge wrote a deeply-felt and moving tribute to him, which is partly an incantation around the word 'Finished':

> Finished: the romances, dark lips and golden eyes...
> Finished: the paprika dishes and the slightly rough red wine shared with beggars while swapping tall tales...
> Finished: the books written...
> Finished: the insults.
> They did not stint there.

The poem ends:

> I am listening in your stead,
> what radiant silence falls on the clamor.

* * *

Serge's long, panoramic novel, *The Long Dusk* is the story of a different kind of exile, this time about a disparate group of refugees who think they have found refuge in Paris, but are forced to flee once again once when German occupation is imminent. Simon Ardatov, a Russian physician, banned from working in France as a doctor, is forced to make a living of sorts working for a scientific cuttings agency. A man who had 'stood under the gallows without trembling', he is now in fear of his landlady demanding the rent, and his brown suit is presentable only in certain, inelegant areas of the city. Pepe Ortiga, a young refugee from the Spanish civil war, had witnessed the 'senseless massacre' at Teruel, and seen 'in a week more bodies than a man should see in a lifetime'; his smoldering black eyes looked out with insolence at the world. And Moritz Silber(stein), a minor wheeler dealer, his affability was intolerable, took his rent payments lightly.

The novel brilliantly conveys the moods of fear and panic, the unbearable tension, as people await the inevitable French capitulation, and yet hope it somehow doesn't happen. Shops start to close up and overloaded cars start to leave the city. Some are driven to suicide. Others wrap up important or valuable books and bury them. There are some who carry on as though nothing has happened. And there are always those who welcome the new rulers. 'Well, the medicine's been swallowed. It feels better now, doesn't it?' says one woman. The Jewish area of the city has become an 'asylum for the wretched of all nations'.

The swift, and violent, Germanization of the city is well-evoked:

Several cities, several different and mutually hostile lives were super-imposed, one upon the other. There were the military staffs, the pleasures of the military staffs, the whisperings of government intrigues, the surveillances ...There was espionage, counter-espionage, commissions, sub-commissions, inspections, secret police in factories, banks, offices, railroad stations ... reports, memoranda, dossiers, classifications, planning, Order. There were perilous clandestine traffickings, messages to prisoners, liberations at a price, mail to the other Zone at ten francs a letter ... Trains rolled eastwards, loaded with machinery and raw materials, luxury articles, Normandy apples, potatoes, furloughed soldiers invigorated by the Paris nights - and in the somber blue light of camouflaged stations, trains full of severe casualties disgorged their loads of the burned and torn, the maimed and the blinded.

And when fuel merchant, Augustin Charras, hero of the First World War, goes for a stroll around the city he loves, which is 'all clean, in mournful Sunday dress', he sees all the signs of the occupation - the swastikas flying from official buildings, the Nazi salutes, soldiers having their photos taken beside the tourist attractions. Chaurras, who 'always seemed to come from far away when spoken to', fears more and more for the safety of his teenage daughter, Angele, whom he sends south. And when he puts himself in danger for hiding a deserter, decides that he too must leave the city.

Ortiga and Ardatov, 'experts in defeat', know the best ways out of the city, the safer routes to the south, but they can do nothing about the new threat to populations on the move, attacks from the air. The highway to Moulins was filled with 'a human river' as all across the country, from 'wounded Champagne and the orchards of Normandy', the roads of France are given over to this movement of human ants heading for escape:

Too many autos riddled with bullets, too many brains still filled with the nightmare of columns of refugees machine-gunned by enormous low-flying planes grazing the treetops, too many families carrying away a cold little body under a blanket ... In the silent night, everyone seemed to hear the droning of distant planes that surely were flying toward this road, capable of spotting these trucks, prepared to let loose meteors of horror.

When they eventually reach the south, there is no safety but only a temporary haven; the exiles have exchanged one form of fear for another and they face the seemingly impossible task of securing papers to leave the country altogether. Serge brilliantly conveys the sheer desperation of people who do not have the right documents, who get over one hurdle just to be faced with another. Leaving the country was never just a question of getting one visa; a whole set of documents had to be put in place, like a suit of cards. One country might well grant a visa, but only to nationals of certain countries; others might grant visas but only for transit and only on proof of onward travel, as well as a visa in place for the final destination. And, of course, papers, authentic or forged, cost money and were usually valid for a short time only: 'The word *visa* could make asthmatics breathe again, relieve sufferers from heart-trouble, cure neuroses, dispel the temptation of suicide; it reigned over condemned horizons as *mirage* reigns over a desert strewn with bones - but this word also wrought devastation, giving rise to diseases of the personality hitherto unknown to psychiatry.'

In this situation, people will go virtually anywhere that will take them, even to countries they haven't heard of. Gaetani, one of the refugees, says, 'I remember the days when we carried a map of the [Paris] Metro around with us. Today, it's the planisphere. Our vision is broadening.'

There are people of all nationalities, from all possible backgrounds, 'Jews of a hundred nations, the last republicans of strangled republics, the last socialists of banned parties, the last revolutionaries of defeated revolutions, the last liberals of conservative democracies ... the last parliamentarians of discredited parliaments ...'

After 30 days waiting, a woman, clutching her handbag, rushes across the square with enough of her wits intact to demand a lethal dose of veronal. Others have not managed to keep their wits intact, like the 'bearded young American, born in

Hungary', who kept 'stamping frantically and shouting in cadence: *Kon-sul ame-ri-cain! Kon-sul ame-ri-cain!*' He is dragged off somewhere, 'No way to shut him up, you couldn't hit an American'.

Ardatov hears of the German attack on Russia and knows that he is now 'doubly hunted', as a Russian and as a communist. He eventually gets French papers, but, knowing he is almost certainly being watched, avoids seeing friends so as not to put anyone remotely at risk, 'Isolation thickened around him.' He had prepared his departure 'as meticulously as a Chinese artisan chisels an ivory charm'. He says goodbye only to Chaurras, who will not leave his country even if he could. Meanwhile, Moritz Silber, has used all his skills to get papers in the name of Silver, a Lithuanian Catholic, and hopes to get to Ecuador. But the possession of papers is no protection against the individuals who have taken it on themselves to inform on people. In this case, he falls victim to the deeply anti-semitic Vibert, the one-time bar-owner. 'Crafty in the performance of duty', Vibert has a fearsome intuition for people who are hiding something and relishes the fact that people called him Viper. Sensing Silber's change of mood to one of hope, once he has secured his false papers, he strikes to deadly effect.

Ortiga finds himself arrested yet again. 'Modern man goes to prison as he takes a train or bus,' he thinks. It's not a problem as long as there is the chance of escape. In prison, he befriends the wonderfully named, Nihil Cervantes, an anarchist who long ago forgot his real name, who offers to share his straw mattress with him. Cervantes tells him they will be sent to build a railway across the Sahara and that, already, he has a plan of escape and invites him to join: 'I know how to say "I am a man friendly to men" in all the languages of the desert and since it's the truth it will get us through wherever we go'. When Ortiga gets a small parcel from Angele, including a tin of sardines, Cervantes takes nothing but some of the oil on a piece of bread, leaving half a sardine for each of the weakest prisoners. (Even though he is faint with hunger, Ortiga wishes he could keep the tin intact because the name, 'Angele', has been scratched on it with a knife.) Ortiga's heroic efforts to keep the malnourished Cervantes alive come to nothing.

Serge brilliantly conveys the endless anxiety of those who have to live in this time. An act as simple or ordinary as opening a door is laden with fear, 'Every time I open the door' Angele says, 'I know that bad news is coming. When someone goes out you can't tell if he's coming back. Or if you open the door, you never know who or what. 'Apart from anything else, being in possession of false papers was a very serious offense. In this time and in this place nothing is certain, 'The planks of safety over the abyss of perdition' seemed perpetually on the point of collapsing. At one point, Moritz Silber sees the trucks loaded with a 'human potpourri', the result of raiding parties:

> The - Jewish - director of an art theatre in Berlin; the - Jewish - correspondent of Amsterdam's (defunct) leading daily; ... the pretty little Catalan girl, who had also escaped - but for love; the aging, crockety German intellectual woman with an expired residence permit; the Tunisian with no papers at all ...; the Viennese - Jewish - psychoanalyst whom this absurd arrest might kill, because his papers would never be in order, because his American visa would expire in a week; the lame, painted widow of a pre-Hitlerian German playwright, looking like a figure in a *danse macabre*; the Italian Freemason who had come to Marseille without a safe-conduct and was wanted by the Armistice Commission ...

And, then at the same time, something wonderful could happen, 'At the very moment of despair a letter arrived bearing stamps from the other world ...'

The novel ends with the start of armed resistance in the area, a resistance which Augustin Charras has decided to join. Serge closes with, 'The end - (but nothing is ended)'.

5

Magicians of word and thought: the Russian cultural revolution

Stupefied, that was the word Serge used to describe his response to the literary revolution that followed the political revolution, 'this glittering debut of Soviet literature ... the audacity and the candor of the writers under a regime barely emerged from the terror'. Small circles of 'young men with hollow cheeks', he wrote, 'wearing the grey greatcoat of the Red Army came together in the evening in very cold (but gold paneled) rooms around poets and prose writers such as Gumilev and Zamyatin, who stoically taught them the art of writing'. This was the time, Serge reminded his readers, 'of the barbed wire fence around Russia, the death of the weak, the conspiracies, the allied intervention, and the war where no prisoners were taken ... This time left us no books. And yet, 'entire galaxies of young writers' sprang up in Russia nevertheless, 'new men shaped by the storm'.

This 'literary renaissance' was the time of novelists like Andrei Bely, Mikhail Bulgakov, Ilya Ehrenburg, Vassily Grossman, Boris Pilnyak, Yevgeny Zamyatin, and Serge himself, as well as the short story writers, Isaac Babel, Andrei Platonov, Varlam Shalamov and Mikhail Zoschenko, and of poets like Anna Akhmatova, Alexander Blok, Osip Mandelstam, Vladimir Mayakovsky, Boris Pasternak and Sergei Yesenin. Also breathtaking was the the revolution in other art forms - painting, architecture, theatre, music and, the still relatively new form of cinema, the men and women involved in these producing the finest work of their lives, people like El Lissitsky, Kasimir Malevich, Lyubov Popova, Alexander Rodchenko and Alexander Tatlin; in theatre, Vsevolod Meyerhold and Constantin Stanislavsky; and in cinema, Alexander Dovzhenko, Sergei

Eisenstein and Dziga Vertov.

Serge wrote a great deal about the writers of the time; his articles, mainly for French leftist journals, constitute a sort of literary history of the period, and he was, often, perceptive and generous.[14] Of Mayakovsky, who is probably today the best known poet of the time, Serge was particularly insightful. He acknowledged his energy and commitment: Mayakovsky did what he said, 'helping the Republic out of the mud, and working as a living poet on the street'. (At demonstrations he would emerge from the crowd to declaim slogans - one of them was 'Lion of Britain, whine!' - some of these poems were 'little master-pieces'.) And in the 'heroic years', he agitated, designed posters, wrote a great work, 'One Hundred and Fifty Million', a unique work, Serge commented, in its 'originality, breadth and power of expression'. And yet even this revealed, in every line, what Serge called 'the internal tragedy of Mayakovsky the Futurist', among other things an overwheening ego; maybe 100 lines start with 'me'. What one was seeing in Mayakovsky's life and work was 'the drama of a poet who could not, in spite of his keen desire to do so, escape from the past'. The fatal flaw of futurism, the artistic doctrine to which Mayakovsky subscribed, was that, despite its name, it was 'tragically linked to the past, in its naive pretense of avoiding it'.

The symbolist poet, Alexander Blok, was Serge said, one of the three or four great lyric poets whom 'nature gives to a privileged people in a hundred years'. He was 'the first, the most admired and the most loved of the master musicians of the Russian language'. Serge praised, in particular, two poems, 'The Twelve' and 'The Scythians', for their understanding of, and support for the revolution. And when he died at only 41, Serge's grief was palpable at the loss of 'one of the magicians of word and thought'.

So too when Andrei Bely was 'devoured' at the age of 53 (in 1934), Serge spoke of him as 'a musician, seeking to give words a sound which were pure, rich and precise'; he possessed all 'the knowledge of the day without it having become a dead letter for him'. Bely's masterpiece, *Petersburg*, published just before the revolution, is now widely regarded as one of the founding works of literary modernism, comparable to Joyce's *Ulysses*. It was very influential on Serge's own writing, especially *Conquered City*. Serge said of his legacy: 'When they have conferred, by the reorganization of everything, a new value on life and on living beings, men will feel quite different and much less powerless in the face of death. But even at this boundary, there is no other hope. Bely knew it better than most of us.'

Of the popular novelist Boris Pilnyak, Serge wrote a long appreciation, which acknowledged his gifts - his originality of talent, his dynamic view of things, the breadth of his outlook and so on - but concluded that the reader was saddened by not finding in him 'anything more than intuitive insight and primitive admiration'.

In the theatre, Serge acknowledged the genius of Vsevolod Meyerhold. Even the propaganda plays he put on, like Mayakovsky's *The Bedbug*, were 'the only great ones', because he still managed to imbue them with 'so frenzied a spirit', that they became something else.

But, of course, this explosion of creativity could not last. There had always been strong currents of philistinism opposed to what these men and women were trying to do, as well as narrow-minded views of what art should be about, especially in a period of revolution These merged in the figure of Stalin who was philistine to his core, denounced anything innovative as 'formalism', and regarded creative artists as tools of the revolution; writers he once famously remarked were 'engineers of the human soul'. For Serge, the key point of the official suffo- cation of creativity was the year 1929. 'There is always an hour,' he wrote, 'when the redeeming choice between cowardice and choice is possible. It was in 1929 that the Soviet writers abdicated their dignity.' Creativity was replaced by 'sterility, of spiritless official propaganda, of stereotypes approved by the bureaus'.

Typically, Serge himself only *started* writing fiction at this point, when he was in his late 30s, after he came close to death in 1928, from an intestinal occlusion. It was also, significantly, the year he was expelled from the Party, which was a different kind of death sentence. Until then, writing of this kind had seemed secondary, but he became increasingly aware of the limitations of historical work which did not permit showing men as they really were, their inner workings and 'penetrating deep into their souls'.

Actual death was the fate of many writers. Isaac Babel, best known for his stories from the civil war, Boris Pilnyak and Meyerhold were all shot. Yesenin and Mayakovsky were driven to suicide, as was the poet, Andrei Sobol. Osip Mandelstam found himself in a camp because of a poem he had written about Stalin which he had shared with a few people only, one of whom betrayed him. He died as a result of his time in prison. The student, Varlam Shalamov, who was involved in distributing Lenin's last testament which had become an illegal document, survived a total of 17 years in prison camps, where he composed the truly shocking stories which would be collected as *Kolyma Tales*, but they were never published in the Soviet Union during his life time.[15]

The price of survival, albeit temporary, for others was public humiliation, as it was for Pilnyak who was forced to rewrite his novel, *Mahogany*. Officially criticized for its 'pessimistic and counterrevolutionary' portrayal of provincial life he had to make it more optimistic, although even this did not save his life, but only deferred his execution. And when he learned in 1937 of Pilnyak's disappearance, Serge remarked that it was not possible to understand from the outside the terrible pressures of a totalitarian regime. One could not, therefore, judge someone because of their 'small retreats, the little acts of pusillanimity' they engaged in to preserve themselves. (As well as being a writer, Pilnyak had been an important publisher, bringing out works by Bely, Babel, Ehrenburg, Yesenin, Mayakovsky, Mandelstam,

Pasternak, Zamyatin, and many others.)

And one hears the sadness when Serge writes in 1937 about the fate of the poet Bezymensky, 'in the flood of terrifying news which comes incessantly to us from Moscow'. One of the most remarkable brains of our younger generation, Serge recalled how ten years before, he had always 'joyfully made his way' to his 'miserable dwelling'. He adapted and maneuvered and became a sort of laureate, even going so far as to praise the execution of Marshal Tukachevsky, the leading Soviet general. But not even this could save him.

Yevgeny Zamyatin was the only writer besides Serge who was allowed to leave the Soviet Union. Ostensibly permitted to go to Paris for medical treatment, he never returned and died there in 1937. Much influenced by HG Wells, of whom he was a great admirer, his novel, We, is an account of a totally controlled, totally administered world, 'the One State', where people have no names, but numbers, and their lives are completely ruled by a principle of rationality. It's a parody of Taylorism, the principle of 'scientific management' (much admired by Lenin): 'such precise beauty: not one superfluous gesture, deviation, turn. Yes, this Taylor was, beyond doubt, the greatest genius the ancients had'. The book ends with the words 'For rationality must conquer.' We, which was translated into English in 1924, was itself a huge influence on Aldous Huxley's Brave New World, and especially on George Orwell.

Others were condemned to artistic silence. Mikhail Bulgakov even wrote to Stalin personally in 1929 asking to be allowed to leave the country if he wasn't allowed to work; he was given some dull work in the theatre as a result. At the same time, he was writing his greatest work, The Master and Margarita. Now universally acclaimed as a masterpiece, in advance of its time, and hugely influential, it was published only in 1966, six years after Bulgakov's death, and even then could only come out abroad. (One of its most quoted lines is 'Manuscripts don't burn'.

Bulgakov himself had burned a version of the book in fear of the consequences; there was no Professor Woland to return it to him with those words, as he does for the Master.)

So too, around this time, Sigizmund Krzhizanovsky was writing *The Letter Killers Club*, but this too was never published in the author's lifetime; few of his writings were. The letter killers are a secret group of 'conceivers' who meet on a Saturday and who, to preserve their conceptions, commit nothing to paper, 'if writers prevent each other from writing, they don't allow readers even to form an idea ... libraries have crushed the reader's imagination'. The group meet in a room with empty bookshelves. Krzhizanovsky was not writing a political allegory but was aiming at something other than that, something metaphysical, and yet he cannot escape the brutal context of his creation, any more than his club can. The book ends, 'The police may pay a visit. Let them: no one searching emptiness has ever managed to find anything'.

Andrei Platonov chose not to write fiction in the early years of the revolution, believing he could serve it better through his practical skill as an electrical engineer. (His first publication was a pamphlet extolling the values of electrification, which would change the nature of work and the nature of humanity.) He started writing fiction in the late 1920s but few of his writings were published. It is only relatively recently that we are able to read him, this man who, according to John Berger, understood 'living modern poverty more deeply than any other storyteller I have come across', a poverty different from others because its 'desolation contained shattered hopes'.

Vassily Grossman, now rightfully acclaimed as a great chronicler of his times, was able to publish some stories in the 1930s, but his monumental masterwork, *Life and Fate*, was seized in 1959 and only published in Switzerland in 1980. Grossman, who had died in 1964, was told his novel could not be published for two or three hundred years. Ilya Ehrenburg abandoned his innovative writing, such as the truly-groundbreaking, *The Life of the*

Automobile (1929), and wrote work which was officially approved of, and even got him a Stalin Prize.

Serge himself was told in 1928 by the director of literary publications, Ilya Yenov, a one-time friend, 'Even if you produce a masterpiece every year, not a line of yours will appear!'. The Russian translation of *Men in Prison*, officially approved, set up to be printed in 10,000 copies, was destroyed. Serge was saved by the fact that he wrote in French and could seek publication abroad, but even this was problematic as he could never be sure that his manuscripts would teach their destinations. He developed the practice of sending detached chapters to France that could be published together, even if some did not arrive!

The great poet Anna Akhmatova was also forced into a kind of silence. Her former husband, Nikolai Gumilev, had been implicated in an anti-Bolshevik plot in 1921 and shot along with 61 others and, even though they had been divorced for three years, this seemed to taint her in the eyes of the authorities. Her later husband, Nikolai Punin, died after many years in the camps; her son was also harassed and imprisoned. She herself would be publicly insulted by Stalin's cultural commissar, Andrei Zhdanov. Although she was unable to publish, she never stopped writing, and her poem sequence, 'Requiem', spoke for many, 'one hundred million voices cry' through her 'tormented mouth'. Akhmatova recalled how, once in a Leningrad prison queue, she was approached by a woman with blue lips who, in a whisper, asked if she would be able to describe 'this', and when she said yes, 'something like the shadow of a smile crossed what had once been her face'.

If the greatest minds were prevented from publishing, the Soviet state, Serge caustically remarked, could make 'almost worldwide reputations' in a few days, for people prepared to do as they were asked, using publicity methods 'borrowed from the American trusts'. The order just had be given to all the sections of the Communist International to have their publishing houses translate a seventh rate work; the entire Communist and Communist-inspired press will proclaim its merits.

In the field of the visual arts, the revolution was, if anything, even more astonishing in its creativity than in literature. The artists Alexander Rodchenko and El Lissitsky were Serge's contemporaries, as was Vladimir Tatlin. Kazimir Malevich and Lyubov Popova were of an older generation, but threw their energies behind the revolution and were far in advance of their time artistically. It was in 1918 that Malevich produced 'Suprematist Composition: White on White', as revolutionary in its own way as much that was happening around him, and which anticipated so-called color field painting by almost four decades.

This artistic freedom was not limited to individual artists but was extended to the whole field of art education. Vkhutemas, the Higher Art and Technical Studios, was the state sponsored school of art set up in 1920, 'to prepare master artists of the highest quali-fications for industry, and builders and managers for professional-technical education'. It was similar in conception to the much better known Bauhaus, set up by Walter Gropius in Weimar in 1919 and forced to close in 1933, many of its staff having gone into exile and the place itself being attacked as degenerate by the Nazis. Like the Bauhaus, Vkhutemas sought to merge the craft tradition with the most modern technology. The constructivist, Alexander Rodchenko, was dean of the metal work faculty. The cubo-futurist painter, Lyubov Popova, taught the use of color. Malevich, advocate of what he called suprematism, taught there, joining the staff in 1925, as did Lissitsky. The textile department was run by the constructivist designer, Varvara Stepanova. At one point it had a teaching staff of 100 and more than 2,500 students. Svomas, free state art studios, were set up in several Russian cities to spread awareness of and competence in the arts to workers and peasants. Entrance examinations were abolished, art history courses were optional, the faculty was replaced by avant-garde artists, and students were free to choose their professors.

Tatlin's monument to the Third International, for which Victor Serge would work in a few years time, was designed at Vkhutemas; never built, perhaps unbuildable, wonderfully grandiose, the dream of a time that refused to be constrained by reality. 'Made of glass, iron and Revolution', Viktor Shklovsky the literary theorist said, while for Mayakovsky it was 'the first monument without a beard'. Taller than the Eiffel Tower, and towering over Petrograd, it would have housed a conference centre, a radio station, a cinema, its different sections revolving at different speeds, the proposal has become an icon and highly influential. (Hints of it can even be seen in Val Myer's Broadcasting House, 1932, in central London.)[16]

Constructivists, like Rodchenko, wanted to make objects that were useful, as well as aesthetically pleasing, from cups and plates and cigarette packets to furniture and social clubs for workers, things that would contribute to the new way of life being constructed. Others, like Lissitsky and Malevich, were more interested in pushing the boundaries of what was aesthetically possible, although early on in his career Lissitsky designed the first post-revolutionary Russian flag and he is also, of course, the creator of the well-known propaganda poster, 'Beat the whites with the red wedge', hugely influential and much replicated, even today.[17]

This was also a period of cross-fertilization in the arts, of breaking down boundaries between different forms. Lyubov Popova, the painter, worked in the theatre with Meyerhold, designing sets for his productions, before her premature death in 1924. Ivan Kudriashev, sent by Malevich to Orenburg in 1919 to set up a branch of Svomas, got involved in doing decorative work for the First Soviet Theater there. Rodchenko and Stapanova worked in theatre too, and Rodchenko also did work for the cinema with Dziga Vertov. He and Lissitsky also designed Mayakovsky's books, and their work influenced generations of book and magazine designers.

There is an awe-inspiring energy about so much of the work in this period, a seemingly endless creativity, astonishing fertility, that, even today, many of the works from this time still seem ready to burst out of their frames, off the paper. One of Lissitsky's greatest compositions, 'Untitled (Rosa Luxemburg)', dedicated to the German revolutionary, murdered in 1919 by paramilitaries, and her body thrown into a canal. is small, and executed with just pencil, brown paper and some gouache. Karel Ioganson's 'Construction', the polar opposite of Tatlin's tower in its quietness and scale, too is just a sheet of paper marked with some ink and colored pencils, while Varvara Bubnova's 'Untitled' of 1920-21, is just ink and brown paper. How much more creative is it possible to be, one wonders, with these materials, at this time?

Of course, it's impossible for us to look at this work now and not be aware that's its time was very short, that by the end of little more than a decade it would all be over. Maybe this is part of what is moving, this brief flowering, this sense of people seizing an opportunity of real freedom, that they know won't come again, to do something useful to the revolution, however they saw it, but without compromising. And of course, it is deeply dismaying to learn that Lissitsky and Rodchenko both ended up, in effect, as propagandists for the regime. Both worked on the official magazine *USSR in Construction*, published monthly throughout the years of the terror and whose main aim was to promote a favorable image of the USSR abroad. Rodchenko even took pictures of slave workers on the White Sea Canal project, a huge propaganda effort to show both the success of the first Five Year Plan, and the use of prison labor as a reforming activity.

As for music, Igor Stravinsky, one of the most important composers of the twentieth century, had left Russia some years before the revolution and was hostile to it when it took place, but he retained a strong artistic connection to the country. He composed some of his most important music of the period for Sergei Diaghilev's Ballets Russes, whose dancers included the legendary Nijinsky and Pavlova, notably *The Firebird* (1910), *Petroushka* (1911) and *The Rite of Spring* (1913), which famously provoked a riot when first performed in Paris. He once quipped that music was 'new just *before* the Soviets', meaning he was the true revolutionary, but this ignored the work of Nikolai Roslavets, a modernist composer who was persecuted for his artistic beliefs, not to mention Dmitri Shostakovich, who in the most challenging personal circumstances, produced a body of work unequalled in its creativity, poetry and humanity. (Fifty years after the revolution, Shostakovich recalled the revolutionary poet, Alexander Blok, in his song cycle, 'Seven Romances'.) It was during this period, too, that Lev Theremin produced the electronic instrument that bears his name today.

In cinema, Sergei Eisenstein's *The Battleship Potemkin* (1925) was hugely innovative and much admired and, indeed, referenced, especially its 'Odessa steps' sequence.[18] Dziga Vertov's *Man with a Movie Camera* (1929), is even more remarkable in its creativity. A documentary without sound about the lives of ordinary people in the Ukraine and elsewhere, the film is celebrated for its use of many technical innovations and it was much influenced by the photomontage techniques being developed by Rodchenko and Lissitsky. So too was Vsevolod Pudovkin's groundbreaking film, *Mother* (1928), based on Maxim Gorky's novel of the same name, about a woman's struggle for justice in pre-revolutionary Russia. Rodchenko and Vertov worked on the journal *Kino-fot* together, and Rodchenko designed posters and tickets for Vertov's films, as well as doing the advertising for Potemkin.[19]

Even in the field of architecture for which, obviously, there was very little scope in a time of extreme shortages, the new order was looking to be as modern as possible. When a trade union body wanted a new headquarters in Moscow it was the great master of modernism himself, Le Corbusier, who they asked to design it. Two years later, however, a competition to build the new Palace of the Soviets in Moscow rejected Corbusier's designs, as it did those of other leading modernists, the preferred design being more bombastic and combined with a memorial to Lenin. (Construction was stopped in 1941 on the outbreak of war.)

Architects found themselves designing buildings for the rapidly expanding secret police. The impressive constructivist Iset Hotel in Ekaterinburg - still in use - was built for the Cheka, and the city also had specially-built accommodation for Cheka staff and their families. Serge notes without a hint of irony that the traveller visiting a commune in the Middle Ages would have stopped to contemplate the belfry tower or the town hall, rising above the poor dwellings of the artisan and the bourgeois. The traveller visiting the cities of the USSR today, 'stops involuntarily, in Moscow, at the top of the Kuznetsky Most, the liveliest artery of the capital, to take in at a glance the latest architectural ensemble, the most imposing edifices of the GPU ... A building of fifteen storeys, huge co-operative stores, dwellings and offices; in the basement and at the rear of vast courts are perfectly silenced prisons; and somewhere behind those facades of fine, polished stone, those shop fronts, those screened windows where the lamplight flares up in the evening, somewhere at the rear of a cellar lighted by neon lights, are the cleverly conceived execution rooms ...

Not even the old palaces of St Petersburg, Serge said, could bear comparison with the new GPU building which dominated the Neva and the Volodarsky Prospect; 'The same is true in all of the centres of the USSR. The most imposing building is that of the GPU.'[20]

And we remember Rodion at the end of *Midnight in the Century* who has found work as a laborer on a secret police building ...

* * *

6

A certain sort of courage: the writer as witness

'This age must be witnessed,' Victor Serge said in his *Memoirs*, 'The witness passes, but his testimony manages to endure - and life still goes on.' Serge was the first of the great historical witnesses of the twentieth century. Witnessing was, for him, 'a means of expressing for people what most of them live without being able to express, as a means of communion, as a testimony about the vast life that flows through us and whose essential aspect we must try to fix for the benefit of those who come after us'. It was something that informed everything he wrote, including his fiction, and was not confined to his reportage, reviews or analysis. Writing was an *act* of solidarity and nowhere is this more true than in his *Memoirs of a Revolutionary*, written in exile in Mexico and, of course, never published in his lifetime.

From the very first lines the reader is captive. Serge tells how, at an early age, he realized that there was no possible escape from the world and yet there was no alternative but to fight for such an escape. He also tells us early on that he learned from the political milieu into which he was born that the only purpose in life was 'conscious participation in the making of history'. On the walls of their apartment were pictures of men and woman who had been executed for their beliefs. (It was a distant relative who had made the bomb used to kill the Tsar, Alexander II in 1881.)

Serge never attended school. Instead his father worked with him, 'not often and not well' he said, but his 'passion for knowledge and the radiance of a constantly armed intelligence', which had never allowed itself to stagnate, or 'to recoil from an inquiry or conclusion', affected him so powerfully, that he was hypnotized by it. Learning was not separate from life, but life itself, and he learned the concrete meaning of words like, 'bread' and 'rent' and 'hunger'. But he also learned at an early age the value of literature as something which could lift people out of the mundane and give real sustenance.

Looking back on his early years, Serge said he had no personal regrets at all; indeed, he said he pitied those who did not know the cruel side of life and the necessity of fighting for mankind. His only regrets were for the energies wasted in struggles which were bound to be fruitless.

Serge had a knack for catching important things in a few words - 'a time of pot-bellied peace' (France and Belgium just before the war), or 'the sudden conversion to fratricidal patriotism' of the German socialists, French syndicalists and anarchists on the outbreak of war in 1914. And when he reached Russia in 1919 to be part of the revolution, it was 'a world frozen to death'; Petrograd was 'the metropolis of Cold, of Hunger, of Hatred, and of Endurance'. Winter itself was 'a torture (there is no other word for it) for the townspeople': no heating, no lighting, and the ravages of famine'. The young and the old were killed in their thousands.

Because of his anarchist and syndicalist past, and independent mind, he was respected by people across the non-Bolshevik left, and because of his literary connections and interests he was known in those circles as a man of culture. As a result, he was often asked to intercede for people who had been arrested; 'The telephone became my personal enemy, at every hour it brought me voices of panic-stricken women'. He also came into contact with many of the key figures in the political and cultural life of the times and he wrote arresting little portraits of them; he was repelled by the affectation and calculated elegance of the poet Yesenin, but he could not resist the 'positive sorcery of that ruined voice'; Georg Lukacs, the Marxist philosopher, 'lived bravely in the general fear', yet would not shake Serge's hand in public (Serge says this with not one note of bitterness); 'a single glance was enough to tell the caliber' of men like Joaquin Maurin and Andres Nin, both teachers who would give their lives for the cause in Spain; the Italian communist, Antonio Gramsci, 'fitted awkwardly into the humdrum of everyday existence, losing his way at night in familiar streets, taking the wrong train' but was intellectually 'absolutely alive'; the US anarchist, Emma Goldman, with 'her organizing flair and practical disposition, her narrow but generous prejudices, and her self-importance'.

Serge's recollections convey, as no one else does, the endlessly appalling conditions, physical and emotional, in Russia from the civil war and war communism onwards, the New Economic Policy, ('The sordid taint of money is visible on everything again'), the slow slide of the country into psychosis (Serge's own word), the arrival of Thermidor, the onset of reaction *from within the bureaucracy*, in November 1927, ('the exhausted Revolution had turned full circle against itself'), the slide also of individuals into despair, ('Nowadays even my friend ... has stopped thinking'). Serge took it upon himself to investigate the desperate underbelly of the society and discovered 'the social inferno', where nothing had changed since Dostoyevsky's time. But when Comintern secretary, Angelica Balabanova, sends through the diplomatic bag, an orange and a bar of soap to Serge and his wife, on the birth of their son, these are 'delicacies from another world'.

Serge watched in hope, as did others, the Chinese revolution begin in 1926. A victory there would have meant the salvation of the Soviet Union, but the official line was that the Communists should accept the rule of the Kuomintang under Chiang Kai-shek. As a result, Communists were massacred in their thousands. With great courage, Serge spoke out against Stalin himself, who had abandoned support for revolutionary movements abroad, because they would destabilize him, by encouraging renewed revolutionary activity in the Soviet Union, and because they would pose external challenges to his dominance in the Communist world.

'Our crime as Oppositionists', Serge wrote, 'lay simply in existing, in not disowning ourselves, in keeping our friendships and talking freely in each other's company'. As the noose around any kind of opposition tightened, he prepared a document which he sent to friends in Paris asking them to publish it if he were to disappear. It was in this that he was the first to describe the Soviet Union as a totalitarian state. And because of his connections with sympathetic people in the bureaucracy, Serge was made aware of the extent to which the Russian secret police and military were collaborating with the Gestapo. A formal pact between the two countries could not be far off. And, of course, he was right.

Today reading *Destiny of a Revolution*, Serge's account of Russia after 20 years, one is struck by the appalling accumulation of evidence about the everyday lives of ordinary Russian people - the food shortages, the alcoholism, the fear, the ruthless oppression of any opposition, however minor, the impoverished public culture - the constant lies, the massive gap between the official version and the lived reality. Serge had an eye not just for the terrible conditions but what they led to; it was terrible that people slept 'in the corridors, in garrets, in lofts, in cellars', but also what these led to, 'the ignorance, the alcoholism and the informing ... the bitter struggles that can occur, for example, over a room whose occupant, an old woman, seems to be on the point of dying', how people were endlessly divided against each other.

Serge brilliantly describes (in *Conquered City*) how letters of denunciation were put together; 'unknown hands, laboring in profound secrecy. Obstinately cut alphabets of all dimensions from the papers, collected them, aligned them on notebook sheets: it would take at least five hundred characters for the contemplated letter.' The patient labor of creating the 'demonic alphabet' is carried out in solitude and in silence. The cut papers then have to be sent with a stone to the bottom of a well, for burning would create smoke and 'where there's smoke there's a fire, don't they say?'

But, for Serge, the greatest evil was not the poverty of means and of men. It was the bureaucratic spirit that prevailed in the schools and which was translated into suspicion, informing, the repetition of formulae devoid of all content, the lessons of pure Stalinism crammed into children eight years old, the stifling of any critical spirit, the repression of all thought, and the hypocritical dissimulation to which the child accustoms himself out of necessity'.[21]

For Serge witnessing wasn't just about reporting something; it was about understanding. So he didn't just describe what was happening, but offered explanations, and these explanations were always drawn from his first-hand experience, his lived knowledge, not just of the material facts which was always considerable, but of the people and the forces involved. Serge would have been the first to admit that the democratic forces within the revolution had, indeed, been roundly defeated very early on, but he was clear about what had brought this about: 'the revolution hemmed in by its foes, undermined at home by Vendees, by conspiracies, by sabotage, by epidemics, by schisms ... the conflict between the battling vanguard of the working-class and its backwards elements, the least conscious and most selfish, those least inclined to sacrifices demanded by the general interest.' In addition there were the activities of dissident groups which served the counter-revolution, for instance the general strike attempted in 1919 by the Mensheviks and social revolu-tionaries, something which would have been suicidal for the revolution. But in the end it was the failure of the revolution to happen anywhere else, especially in Germany, that was to be the decisive factor. Instead of breaking the 'iron circle in which the soviets were suffocating', the revolution faced 'lasting isolation, increased economic difficulties, a moral depression, the weakening of the internationalist revolutionary tendencies, the strengthening of bureaucratic nationalistic, moderating tendencies ...'

Serge was in no way romantic about people; he had had too much experience of personal ambition, betrayal, venality and so on for that. But he was also reluctant to judge, as we saw when he refused to condemn other writers who had maneuvered this way and that to try to save themselves. But he understood, as few people did, the forces at work at particular moments. This is why Serge's account of the Russian revolution is so important today because it stands as a corrective to the popular view that the revolution was somehow fated from the start and, moreover, that this is how all revolutions will end, must end. Not at all, says Serge; there were always choices to be made, courses of action to be decided on. It could have been different. Serge is always also a reminder that one of the reasons the revolution degenerated was the massive external forces ranged against it.

* * *

Daria, in Serge's last novel, *Unforgiving Years*, working as a teacher in a village in Kazakhstan, has been a witness of sorts. But, because of the times in which she lives, her writings have had to be of a strange kind indeed:

A curious document, this journal, whose carefully chosen words sketched out only the outer shapes of people, events, and ideas: a poem constructed of gaps cut from the lived material, because - since it could be seized - it could not contain a single name, a single recognizable face, a single unmistakable strand of the past, a single allusion to assignments accomplished ... No expression of torment or sorrow (this for the sake of pride), no expression of doubt or calculation (for the sake of prudence), and nothing ideological, naturally, for ideology is the sludge at the bottom of the pitfall ...

The construction of the 'featureless record' was like a 'thought puzzle in three dimensions turned entirely toward some undefinable fourth dimension', had become an exhilarating occupation. So there is nothing about the passionate relationship she is having with Klimentii, nothing of the 'surrenders of the flesh, phosphorences of the spirit transmuted into inner riches, she'd had no inkling of before'. Also, she sees that 'no contoured shoulder, no quiver of eyelashes can ever be wholly expressed ...'But even this minimal record is potentially too dangerous for the time and must be burned when she is transferred. Her last act there is to distribute 'her riches', some bread and sugar and a bar of rose-scented soap which she carves into slices so it can be distributed more fairly.

Once in Leningrad, Daria is shocked at how even the buildings seem to have aged by 'a couple of centuries in a few short seasons', just as the men and women 'looked decades older in only a few months', while the children had 'aged a lifetime before knowing what life was'. But it is what she sees in people's faces when they glance at her that disturb her even more. She has never seen this before; it is not the gaze of the hungry:

> ...this look was inexpressibly different from the looks of the past. She hadn't known that eyes could change so, and cry out so loudly in silence something intolerable. It was neither pain, nor hallucination ... What were all those eyes saying? That they had weathered day and night, indefinitely, the storms of snow and terror, of filth, exhaustion, cold, hunger, fright, sickness, with no hope of escape, no hope of healing ... That they were watching life die away within themselves.

She sees the dead being transported, each corpse tied to a sled pulled on a string by its next of kin; a 'new breed of resourceful specialists' earned their food by sewing discarded sheets or squares of sackcloth around the remains. Daria passed several 'such mummies on the street. Rigid pods floating just above the trodden snow. A living man or woman to pull the string, and sometimes a child behind ...'

This part of the novel ends with Daria saving the life of a neighbor by giving her last

vodka, vitamins, 'a tin of fish in brine, the half-eaten bar of stale chocolate', and then going home to face her own feelings that she, too, is beginning to die, 'Hunger and loneliness, two tentacles of death'.

The third section of the novel, 'Brigitte, Lightning, Lilacs', is a stunning achievement of witnessing. It is a shocking picture of Germany during the final days of the war, when the country has become a waste land, devastated by aerial bombardment, as well as by the war on the land; a country laid waste, where not only topography has been destroyed, cities flattened, landmarks destroyed, but time too has been altered, the future itself has been wiped out, 'the old was obliterated forever'.

Richard Greeman points out in his introduction that Serge was in advance of his time in showing the Germans as themselves victims, something that was unthinkable until relatively recently, when it has become possible to acknowledge the horrors afflicted on ordinary Germans, as in the fire-bombing of cities like Dresden which had no strategic purpose but was designed purely to terrify, and also the use of mass rape of women by Russians, again as a form of terror. But when Serge was writing, in the years just after the war, this was a courageous act, another gesture of solidarity with the victims of history.

Serge evokes the fear that is always present: 'There were daylight raids, nighttime raids, twilight raids, dawn raids, and errors in the warning system, which announced a bombing raid when it had already begun and sounded the all-clear as it was starting over again'.

Serge himself, of course, had spent time in Germany in the 1920s, working for the Comintern and had lived among these people. To him, they were not some faceless enemy, but real men and women, many of whom had thoughts and ideas similar to his own, and who had come very close to making their own socialist revolution. Brigitte of the section title is not a Nazi, but from a social democratic family, and her fiancé, a soldier, we learn, has himself been executed along with the rest of his tank crew, because of their 'bad attitude', in not supporting the war wholeheartedly. 'A desert is what we have made', he says to her in one of his letters. He describes what it is to like to ride over a group of men who have been hiding in the snow - 'they screamed like mice being crushed' and the tank treads are clogged with bleeding flesh. He also tells her how his unit attacked an enemy tank, even though they wished to surrender. He watches a blonde 20 year old burning, 'I watched his face twist like a paper mask tossed onto a bonfire'.

He, too, has had to become a witness. He tells Brigitte, 'I had to see it all, since I'm the observer ... I told myself: Look at what you're doing, you must look without blinking, you're not allowed to close your eyes'. He vividly describes the gradual brutalization that he sees taking place in his fellow soldiers. Fear, he says with some insight, comes from a surprise inflicted on the imagination, 'Once the surprise has worn off, a hanged man seems perfectly natural'. There were so many, they no longer frightened anyone. 'Was it necessary to unleash hell on earth', he asks.

And for Gunther, who has brought Brigitte the letters, 'the only natural coupling is a rape in the barn of some smoldering farm', as he recalls the 'skinny black-haired Slovene' who had tried to hide under some sacks and then opened her mouth to scream, but didn't because others were already doing so. Serge paints an appallingly vivid picture of the inferno that Germany has become:

Thunderclaps sent huge waves through the earth, crackling

outbursts transmuted into great surges of heat, as though invisible ripples of fire were pulsing outward from a fiery oven, somewhere nearby, to one side, deep underground. "We're going to be baked like potatoes in ashes," an old man calmly remarked ... The earth shuddered, smoke crept across it, people dwelt in a volcanic realm of sudden explosions, smoldering dormant fires, smoky eddies of soot, dust clouds, the stench of reeking corpses, charred and splintered trees that persisted in budding and even put out, here and there, tender pale-green leaves as though nothing were amiss.

Life continues, just as the lilac bushes tended by Herr Schiff, the schoolteacher, have survived the heat and the dust, 'The force of simple vegetal vitality. 'Schiff goes back into his house and finds a pillow case which he ties to a ruler and puts it above the door: 'Already white rags were flocking across the ruins, some floating with the gay flutter of doves. As far as the eye could see, the whole city was covering itself with white birds, captives who would never take wing.'

* * *

Serge would be followed as a witness by people such as Nadezhda Mandelstam, widow of the poet, Yevgenia Ginzburg and Alexander Solzhenitsyn who reported, in their own brave ways, from that same place of desolation. And of course Primo Levi, *the* witness of the Shoah, who, in *If This is a Man*, *The Truce*, *The Drowned and the Saved* and other books, dared to speak of the unspeakable, all the time reminding us that the real witnesses, 'those who saw the Gorgon', were dead; he and other survivors were the exception, an anomaly. It was this which haunted him till he too joined them. And let's remember too that Levi was not always the hugely popular and widely-read figure he became. When he first wrote about his experiences, no major publisher was interested in his book and, when eventually published by a small imprint, it quickly went out of print. People did not want to know.

I think too of Eduardo Galeano, the self-described 'Magical Marxist - one half reason, one half passion, a third half mystery' - who, in his massive counter-history of the Americas, *Memory of Fire*, as well as in other books like *Mirror* and *The Book of Embraces*, has redefined the writing of history, mixing historical fact, popular myth, fiction and poetry, to achieve a deeper truth. I think also of Simon Leys, the Sinologist who became a political commentator in the 1960s and 1970s, only because no one else seemed willing to do it. Indeed, Leys compares the refusal of the Western media to hear the truth about what was happening in Mao's China with Serge's experience regarding Stalin's Russia. Leys remarks that his sources were invariably public, and that his only expertise was his knowledge of Chinese, as well as knowing *how* to read what is said and not said, crack the code of the official jargon, the 'secret language full of symbols, riddles, cryptograms, hints, traps, dark allusions, and red herrings.'[22]

But of all the writers who have followed, it was the Spanish Communist, Jorge Semprun, who most embodied the legacy of Serge. Like Serge he came from a political family; his father was the Spanish republic's ambassador to the Netherlands, although his maternal grandfather had been the Conservative prime minister, Antonio Maura. Born in Madrid in 1923, Semprun lived in France after the defeat of the Republic, was a member of the Spanish Communist Party in exile. With the German occupation, he joined the resistance, was arrested in 1943 and sent to the concentration camp at Buchenwald. The five day train journey there would provide the framework for his first novel, *Le Grand Voyage*, translated as *The Cattle Truck*, which won the 1963 Formentor prize. Semprun was presented with copies in 12 languages, but the Spanish edition, being specially set up in Mexico, hasn't yet arrived, is blank, 'Finally, I feel moved.'

Semprun's allocation to the camp work administration, effectively run by the Communists there, along with his fluency in German, almost certainly ensured his survival. Bizarrely, horribly, it was this work that would lead many former camp inmates later to fall under suspicion, sometimes fatal, after the war was over. Josef Frank, a leading Czech Communist, found himself in the dock in Prague accused of being a war criminal and a Nazi collaborator. He was hanged a few days later and his ashes scattered 'on the snow somewhere around Prague, so that no trace of his passage on earth would remain'.

It was his experience at Buchenwald that Semprun used as the centre for his fictionalized memoir, *What a Beautiful Sunday* (1983). Semprun was, of course, familiar with Goethe's visits to the area the previous century with his friend, the poet Eckermann: 'Not without some degree of intellectual perversity, I was pleased to imagine Goethe's conversation with Eckermann on the subject of the Buchenwald camp. What would Goethe have said if he had noticed, as he walked along the Avenue of Eagles, one December Sunday, for instance, the wrought-iron inscription on the monumental camp gates, Jeden das Seine, TO EACH HIS DUE?. The book begins with the narrator, who has strayed from the area permitted to inmates, gazing at a beech tree from the camp when, behind him, he hears a German officer cocking his pistol, getting ready to kill him. In response to the question what is he doing there, he thinks for a second and says, 'Das Baum, so ein wunderschones Baum.' He then jumps to attention and shouts his number in German, 'Haftling vier-und-vierzig-tausend-neun-hundert-vier', which probably saves his life. 'Between SS Warrant Officer Kurt Krauss and No. 44904 there is all the distance created by the right to kill.'[23]

After the war, Semprun became a translator for Unesco, but started working clandestinely in Spain for the Communist Party in 1953, an activity he would carry on courageously for many years. How dangerous the work was shown by the fact that

Semprun's replacement was arrested, tortured and executed. He was also member of the party central committee and of the Politburo. His account of this period of his life, *The Autobiography of Frederico Sanchez*, his *nom de guerre*, won the prestigious Planeta prize in 1977.[24] But Semprun became increasingly critical of the Party's position, as it more and more lost touch with what was actually happening in Spain. He, and his friend Fernando Claudin, would eventually be denounced at an executive committee meeting in Moscow by the legendary 'La Pasionaria' (Dolores Ibarrurri) as 'feather-brained intellectuals', and expelled from the Party. (Semprun also used this experience for the screenplay of Alain Resnais' subtle and compelling 1966 film, *La Guerre est Finie*, although he is probably better known for his work with Costa-Gavras.)

In many ways Semprun and Serge could not have been more different. Semprun was from a well-off family, had an elite education, and was an uncritical, orthodox Communist for many years; he said himself he did *not want* to know the truth of Soviet Russia and elsewhere. When he did confront the truth, as he did when he wrote the screenplay for Costa-Gavras' 1970 film, *L'Aveu* (*The Confession*) about the Czech show trials, he did so with an unrivaled power. With Serge, he shared an emotional honesty - 'There is no such thing as an innocent memory. Not for me any more.' he wrote, as well as humanity and courage. And like Serge, Semprun had postponed his writing, preferring political activity to the word. Hence the title he chose for his memoir, *Litterature ou la vie*, although as someone remarked, this really ought to have been translated as *Writing or Life*. Above all, they shared a commitment to truth and to witnessing for others, and it was always in the service of these that they wrote.[25]

7

Shared veins: hope and the soul

Serge was in no way a personal writer; there is very little ego in his writing and this is true even of the *Memoirs*. He has a very clear sense of what is private and what is public. When he writes that the worst intimacy of prison was not that of bodies, although that wass awful, but 'not being able to be with yourself ... to remove your face from the prying glance of others', we see what a torment this was to a private man. The word 'I' was, he once said, repellent to him, 'a vain affirmation of the self which contains a large measure of illusion and another of vanity or unjustified pride'. He preferred to think instead of a 'we', as his experience illuminated that of the people, 'to whom I feel tied'. Unlike the 'we' of Zamyatin's dystopia in which the individual does not exist, Serge's 'we' is the ground, the context of individuality. It is this sense of a real connection to, and authentic communion with, others, a deep humanism, always on the side of the powerless but which never slides into sentimentality, that gives his work much of its power. For his prose is of a piece with that view, always congruent He had a rare ability to convey things powerfully in ordinary language, without any obvious artifice, literary conceit or stylishness. There is not one word that sends the reader to the dictionary, or a formulation whose meaning is not clear to the attentive reader.

And he was always writing about real people, never about abstractions. This was much rarer on the left at the time he wrote than it ought to have been. It is this that makes books like *From Lenin to Stalin* and *Destiny of a Revolution* engaging still, 75 years after he wrote them. This short passage from *Conquered City* about conditions in the countryside, merges both the awful facts of what is happening, with the terrible personal consequences,

'So began the black years. First expropriated, then deported, some seven per cent of the farmers left the region in cattle cars amid the cries, tears, and curses of urchins and disheveled women and old men mad with rage. Fields lay fallow, cattle disappeared, people ate the oil cake intended for the stock ...'

* * *

One of the things that gives depth to Serge's understanding of people was his belief in the soul. This was unusual for someone who was in no way religious and probably had a lot to do with the anarchism, with which he had grown up, and which formed him politically. Whatever its roots, Serge had always believed in, what he called, a 'materialist spirituality'. 'The immaterial,' he wrote in his notebook, 'is not in the least unreal' even if it was 'unexplainable by yesterday's scientific rules'. And the soul, for him, was an embodied soul, 'The soul would be nothing if it were not flesh.'

Serge's interest in these matters was deepened by his friendship in exile in Mexico with the German psychiatrists, Fritz Fraenckel and Hubert Lennhof, both veterans of the German socialist movement and the Spanish civil war. Fraenckel, who was once mistaken by a waitress for Einstein, believed that Freud's thinking was equal to that of Marx with its 'new revelations' of man. Their conversations touched on the role of character and personal psychology in the beginning of the conflict between Trotsky and Stalin, as well as the psychological roots of Nazism and the emotional foundations of totalitarianism. The two men would discuss their dreams on the bus.[26] Serge wrote in his notebook:

Men are psychological beings; impossible to act with them, on them, without taking this fact into account, in the most serious sense of the definition. Socialist schematism didn't ... take their souls into account ... 'No psychology!' I heard this little sentence thousands of times in Russia. It meant, 'We're fighting, we're working, efficiency first, material objectivity!' and it came out of the most narrow-minded industrial pragmatism ... The striking thing is that the Russian Revolution came to an end through a psychological drama. The whole of contemporary history revolves round that drama and around the Nazi phenomenon which is both economic and psychological at one and the same time ... Psychology will perhaps be the revolutionary science of totalitarian times; socialism will no longer be able to do without it without lowering itself and reducing itself to a kind of sterility.

These are private notes only, written for himself, but we can see Serge groping towards something important, a whole dimension of being human, one which had been fatally missing from the socialist project. Even if he never theorized it, it was always present in what he wrote, that socialism was not about abstractions, but about real people, and it is real people who inhabit his writing.

Serge knew of psychologist Bruno Bettelheim's courageous article on how different individuals responded to the terrible shock of finding themselves thrown into concentration camps, based on his observations while himself an inmate in Dachau and Buchenwald.[27] He also reviewed the Marxist psychoanalyst, Erich Fromm's, pioneering 1941 book, *Escape from Freedom*, welcoming it as a 'valuable contribution to what might be called our "intellectual rearmament"'. Agreeing with Fromm that people accepted authoritarian regimes partly because they were afraid of their own freedom, Serge argued that totalitarian regimes created, in turn, a new kind of insecurity, 'even worse than the one it remedied'; Germans and Russians now lived in a state of 'permanent catastrophe'.[28] And Serge had seen in his own life what persecution could do to individual people; his wife Liuba Russakova had been driven mad by it; on one occasion, offered a cup of tea by the writer, Boris Pilnyak, she thought she was being poisoned. She spent time in psychiatric clinics in

Russia (where the secret police were active) and in France, where, tragically, she had to be left behind when Serge and their children went to Mexico. She died in 1985.

* * *

Serge was not an optimist; he never saw silver linings in the dark clouds, never believed that everything would somehow turn out for the best. Not for him the 'optimism of the will', advised by Gramsci, even if combined with the 'pessimism of the intellect' (whatever that might mean). What he did have was *hope*, which is something different, and which always carries within it the possibility of disappointment. And unlike optimism, which is just a kind of wishful thinking, hope is based on experience, and, for Serge, this was not just his own but the experience of history, that people would always strive for a better life: 'The course is set on hope', as he ended one of his poems in exile.

Another contemporary, the free-thinking Marxist philosopher, Ernst Bloch, devoted much of his life to documenting the many manifestations of what he called, 'the principle of hope'. This was evident, Bloch argued, in a great deal of culture, from fairy tales to popular songs, to drama and opera. Unlike the Freudian unconscious which was directed to the past, what Bloch called the 'Not-Yet-Conscious', was disposed 'towards the side of something new that was dawning up'. It was the utopian element in human culture, utopian in the sense of what Bloch called the 'forward dream', the hope for, and anticipation of, something better. Human beings, Bloch argued, were not just beings who craved or had needs, but were beings capable of wishing, and it is this wishing, whether for something personal or something social, that gives rise to desire and hope. (It was this that Marx himself had in mind when he spoke of the 'dream of the matter' that the world had long ago possessed but which it did not know how to bring into being.)

Strangely, it is precisely Serge's hopefulness, Susan Sontag remarked with some insight, that has contributed to his marginality. His work, she said, 'refused to take on the expected cargo of melancholy'. This, she implies, is much preferred, particularly on the left. Sontag brings to mind another of Serge's contemporaries, Walter Benjamin, and about whom she had herself written a perceptive and moving article, where she spoke of his 'unquenchable gloom'. The contrast between the two men is striking. A small industry has grown up around the figure of Benjamin. There have been biographies, a film, endless commentaries, even novels and an authorized collected works, now in several volumes. There is also a major memorial at the place of his death.

The difference between the reception of the two men is not hard to understand. Benjamin is the man of almost pure theory and, as such, the kind of man feted in our time with its love of 'theoretical practitioners'. (The fact that he was also more than a little mystical in his thinking adds a certain exoticism.) The manner of his death in September 1940 has lent weight to the myth: the hard, and painful, trek over the Pyrenees, the loss of a briefcase with an unpublished manuscript, 'more precious than my life', suicide by poison in a hotel room in Port-Bou when he feared he would be sent back to certain death.

I have no wish here to deny Benjamin's importance, or the value of his thought. His essay on the work of art in the age of mechanical reproduction was genuinely groundbreaking, although even he could not have foreseen that the photograph, which he thought was displacing the original work of painting, would itself become a commodity, despite being, as he remarked, 'infinitely reproducible'. It's impossible also to forget, once encountered, the figure of the angel of history, even if it doesn't really stand up to too much scrutiny. And impossible, too not to be charmed by the idea of this man, the most exacting of intellectuals, doing a series of radio broadcasts for children! Nor do I wish to deny the terrible personal tragedy of his death, but simply to note the acute disparity between the after-lives of the two men.

(Serge did, of course, also write theoretically but, to my mind, this was not his strength. Serge writing about individual writers, like Blok or Mayakovsky, is far more interesting than Serge developing a theory of the proletarian novel.)

* * *

It is in his hopefulness, that Serge makes me think of John Berger, who has himself sustained hope for very many years, in everything he has done. Himself a long-time and insightful admirer of Serge, as we saw earlier, Berger has always been on the side of the oppressed, not just in his active solidarity with the powerless from Mexico to Gaza, but in his writing. Whatever the form he has inhabited - he has been novelist, poet, artist, critic, film-maker - he has been a storyteller, often in powerful collaboration with others, 'against the great defeat of the world'. His has been a persistent voice, intransigent and angry but also compassionate, that a more just ordering of the world is, not just desirable, but possible. His belief in the power of art has sustained many, whether in his understanding of poetry, with its echoes of Serge, as a secular form of prayer against the cruelty and indifference of the world, or the other voices he has, through his generous celebration, helped make known, like Anne Michaels, Juan Gelman, Andrei Platonov, or the work of the artists he has championed and helped us to appreciate, like Giacometti, Zadkine, Leger, Juan Munoz. This is why so many people feel they have this direct relationship with him, as though he is writing to and for each one of us. This is what makes a book, like *Bento's Sketches* (2011), which takes, as its starting point, the lost sketchbook of a seventeenth-century philosopher (!), with its drawings of a cat sleeping, a dead badger, some flowers, people in Berger's life, its stories of exile, its meditations on art and the state of the world, so inspiring, like a message of hope. 'Some fight because they hate what confronts them;' Berger wrote many years ago, 'others because they have taken the measure of their lives and wish to give meaning to their existence. The latter are likely to struggle more persistently.' These words about another contemporary of Serge, Max Raphael, the German Marxist art critic, he might equally have said of Serge himself.

* * *

Serge also never forgot that human beings lived in a physical world. Just as there was never an 'I' who was outside of a 'we', so we humans, by definition, inhabited a natural world that is not of our making, that has been given to us. This was a constant source of wonder to him, as well as sustenance, and he never stopped celebrating it. Remember the tree bark the prisoners liked to touch, or the pebbles to hold, or the arrival of spring, or the sunlight on the exiles' faces. Or the lilac that survives the endless bombing. Here is a short passage from *Birth of Our Power*, which is like a little prose poem:

> The blue waters mirror a pure sky in their shimmering silk folds. Invisible strings tremble on the burning air like the flight of bee swarms. The light hums. In the distance are white sails. Flights of seagulls describe curves of whiteness which fade like a light caress in the crystal blue air. The rocks of Montjuich are tinted with amber.

And it is the 'splendidly simple world' of nature that Daria is delighted to find herself connected to, once again, in the final section of his last novel, *Unforgiving Years*. Like Serge, Daria has found a refuge of sorts in Mexico and, standing in her yard in early morning, she sees:

Purple sprays of bougainvillea poured over the broken walls. A thicket of menacing nopals - fleshy green - bristled vehemently, and they bore bulbous flowers of a delicate red. A yellow campanile rose above its surround of tall trees, hairy with creepers trailing from every branch. The brightness of the morning was expanding into a vivid symphony of color that promised to intensify almost beyond endurance after this hour of exquisite softness. A monumental joy ... conjoined earth and sky in the embrace of the light.

* * *

It is true that Serge's hope was, at times, misplaced. He greatly underestimated the power of Stalinism and its successors. Stalin was removed from power, not by a rebellion of those he subjugated, as Serge had imagined he would be, but only by death, in March 1953, while The authoritarian state itself remained in place foralmost a half century after Serge, and countless others, had hoped for its demise; the statue of Felix Dzerzhinsky, first head of the Cheka, remained in the feared Lubyanka Square until 1989. But the regimes were not unchallenged. Many people recall the Prague Spring and Poland's Solidarity movement, but we need to remember, too, the uprisings in East Germany in 1953, in Hungary in 1956, in Poland in 1970, all unbelievably courageous, all ruthlessly crushed.

Particularly in the wake of the collapse of the Soviet empire in 1989, so much has been talked about a supposed end of history. But history is never over; it is always in the making, and people still hope for a better world, for a better future, in which they can be the subjects, not the objects of their lives, and they are prepared to give life itself for it. This much, at least, must be clear from recent events in the Arab world, and not only there.

Wherever they are, people are constantly trying to change their lives, to challenge oppression. They may not do so under the banner of socialism, far less communism - has an idea ever been so twisted out of meaning as this one? - but they still want something other than what they have. I'm reminded of the words of William Morris about people fighting for something and when it comes about is not what they meant, 'and other men have to fight for what they meant under another name'.

So Serge's words about conscious participation in the making of history, of being on the side of all that enlarges human beings and against what diminishes them, and of just requiring a certain sort of courage to speak the truth, are as vital today as they ever have been.

* * *

The last word he wrote, *Dazzling*.

Writings by Victor Serge

Novels

Men in Prison, 1930, translated by Richard Greeman, 1969.

Birth of Our Power, 1931, translated by Richard Greeman, 1967.

Conquered City, 1932, translated by Richard Greeman, 1975.

Midnight in the Century, 1939, translated by Richard Greeman, 1982.

The Long Dusk, 1946, translated by Ralph Manheim, 1946.

The Case of Comrade Tulayev, 1948, translated by Roger Trask, 1950.

Unforgiving Years, 1971, translated by Richard Greeman, 2008.

Short stories

Le Tropique et le Nord, 1972, translated by John Manson at http://www.pennilesspress.co.uk

Poetry

Resistance, 1938, translated by James Brook, 1986.

Political writings

Carnets, 1985, translated by John Manson at http://www.victorserge.net.

Collected Writings on Literature and Revolution, translated and edited by Al Richardson, 2004.

Destiny of a Revolution, translated by Max Shachtman, 1937. (Sometimes published as *Russia: twenty years after*.)

From Lenin to Stalin, translated by Ralph Manheim, 1937.

Memoirs of a Revolutionary, translated by Peter Sedgwick, 1963. (New edition with restored material, 2012.)

Revolution in Danger: writings from Russia 1919 -1921, translated by Ian Birchall, 1997.

What Every Radical Should Know About State Repression, anonymous translation, nd.

Witness to the German Revolution: writings from Germany 1923, translated by Ian Birchall, 1997.

Year One of the Russian Revolution, translated by Peter Sedgwick, 1972.

Further reading

(The literature on Serge is now substantial; these are the things I've found most interesting.)

Murray Armstrong, 'The searchers', *Guardian*, 22 September 1990.

John Berger, 'Victor Serge', *Selected Essays and Articles: the look of things*, Penguin, 1972.

Julian Gorkin, 'The last years of Victor Serge, 1941-47', *Revolutionary History*, vol. 5, no. 3, autumn 1994.

Richard Greeman, Introductions/afterwords to the individual novels.

-: 'The Victor Serge affair and the French literary left', http://www.marxists.org/history/etol/revhist/backiss/vol5/no3/greeman.html

-: 'Victor Serge and the novel of revolution', http://www.marxists.de/culture/greeman/sergenovel.htm

James Hoberman, 'Orphan of history', *New York Review of Books*, 22 October 2009.

Bill Marshall, *Victor Serge: the uses of dissent*, Berg, 1992.

Susan Sontag, 'Unextinguished: the case for Victor Serge', Introduction to 2004 NYRB edition of *The Case of Comrade Tulayev*, also in *At the Same TIme: essays and speeches*, Penguin Books, 2008.

Susan Weissman, *Victor Serge: the course is set on hope*, Verso, 2001.

Debt to translators

English language readers of Victor Serge are inevitably indebted to his many translators; without them his work simply would not exist. We are particularly indebted to Richard Greeman and to Peter Sedgwick, not just translators but partisans, key members of what Serge's French publisher, Francois Maspero called, the 'secret international of Serge admirers', trying to make sure he is given his rightful place in the world.

Thanks also to Ian Birchall, James Brook, Max Eastman, Ralph Manheim, John Manson, Al Richardson, Roger Trask and the, sadly anonymous, translator of *What Every Radical Should Know about State Repression*. Thanks, too, to the many small publishers who have done so much in the face of commercial adversity to keep Serge in print, in particular, Francis Boutle, Bookmarks, Haymarket, Journeyman, Pluto Press, Redwords and Writers and Readers.

Endnotes

1   For Gorkin's account see, 'The last years of Victor Serge, 1941-47', *Revolutionary History*, vol. 5, no. 3, autumn 1994.

2   Paz speaks of Serge in his memoir, *Itinerary: an intellectual journey* (trans, Jason Wilson), Harcourt, New York, 1999.

3   I still find it difficult to use the word 'soviet' in anything other than its true meaning - the workers' councils and factory committees thrown up in the revolution as expressions of genuine popular power. They were opposed by the Bolsheviks as early as late 1917, and eventually dominated by them. (See Maurice Brinton, 'The Bolsheviks and Workers' Control', in *For Workers' Power: the selected writings of Maurice Brinton*, edited by David Goodway, AK Press, 2005). The word also came, especially in the mouths of US politicians and military people, to be a term of cold war abuse: 'the soviets' were the enemy. As for the Union of Soviet Socialist Republics, 'four words, four lies', the great, and greatly-missed, political and social theorist, Cornelius Castoriadis, once quipped, according to Milan Kundera.

4   John Berger, 'Victor Serge', in *Selected Essays and Articles: the look of things*, Penguin, 1972, pp. 75-77; Christopher Hitchens, 'Victor Serge: pictures from an inquisition' in *Arguably*, Atlantic Books, 2011; Susan Sontag, 'Unextinguished: the case for Victor Serge', Introduction to 2004 NYRB edition of *The Case of Comrade Tulayev*, also in *At the Same TIme: essays and speeches*, Penguin Books, 2008.

5   Davd Widgery, *The Left in Britain 1956-68* Penguin, 1976; Andy Marino, *American Pimpernel*, Century Hutchinson, 1999, p. 224; John Leonard, *The Last Innocent White Man in America*, New Press, 1993, p 124.

6   In the middle of the previous century the great Russian writer Dostoyevsky had spoken of his own imprisonment in

similar terms. Having served four years for his part in a political conspiracy, Dostoyevsky wrote to his brother, that he felt he had 'been buried alive and shut up in a coffin ... it was an indescribable and unending agony, because each hour, each minute weighed upon my soul like a stone'. Dostoyevsky too would write a novel, *The House of the Dead*, to come to terms with his experience.

7   The embassies and military missions of the Allies were, in reality, 'centers of permanent conspiracy', as Serge describes them in his report on state repression, where counter-revolutionaries of all kinds 'found subsidies, weapons, political direction'. One of those active against the revolution was the British diplomat and spy, Robert Bruce Lockhart, who was eventually arrested. He was one of those whose freedom was being negotiated for in exchange with the camp inmates in France, who included Serge.

8   The story is recounted in Susan Weissman, pp.210-213.

9   Serge's researches were first published in France in 1926 as *Les Coulissses d'une Surete Generale: ce que tout revolutionnaire doit savoir de la repression*. Various editions have been published since, usually dropping the title and using only the sub-title, *What every radical should know about state repression*, which gives a rather misleading idea of the book's contents. (The first edition I came across was published by one of the more paranoid groups on the far left.)

10   The Cheka, or Extraordinary Commission, created in 1917 by Lenin, was reorganized in 1922 as the State Political Directorate or GPU, of the NKVD, the People's Commisariat for Internal Affairs.

11   In his short story, 'The Leningard Hospital', Serge showed how the network of repression extended to the psychiatric system. The patient, Iouriev, has been admitted for a strange misfortune indeed, because he has overcome fear. His psychiatrist explains:

"Iouriev, humble citizen of our times, was ravaged by it for a long time, like you and me. The workers, he explains, are afraid of dying of hunger it they don't steal, afraid of stealing, afraid of the Party, afraid of the Plan, afraid of themselves. The guilty are afraid to own up, the innocent are afraid of their innocence and of having nothing to confess. The intellectuals are afraid of understanding and afraid of not understanding, afraid of seeming to understand or not seeming to understand ... The people are afraid of the authorities and the authorities are afraid of the people ... the men of the Politburo are afraid of each other, afraid to act, afraid not to act ... The Leader is afraid of his subordinates, his subordinates are afraid of him ... The revelation came to Iouriev one morning. He woke up, delivered. No fear of anything - anything. The very illumination of feeling clean. He felt he had no right to keep the secret to himself so he spent several days writing forty Appeals to the People ... He spent a night sticking them up in the centre of the city, under the eyes of the militia and belated passers-by. They took him for an ordinary bill-poster who was working a little late to have more peace and quiet. And he went home to bed. The next morning he is arrested but his suitcase is already packed."

Serge was here anticipating the practice whereby the Soviet state would declare 'insane', dissidents and opponents, an abuse of psychiatry that was condemned worldwide. Prominent figures treated in this way included the poet Joseph Brodsky, the scientists Zhores Medvedev and Andrei Sakharov, and people like Natalya Gorbanevskaya who, with unbelievable courage, demonstrated, with a handful of others, in Red Square against the Soviet invasion of Czechoslovakia in 1968.

The story is probably the only work of his to have been adapted for the screen; an adaptation, directed by Sarah

Maldoror, was broadcast on French TV in 1983. The cast included Rudiger Vogler, best known for his work in several Wim Wenders films.

12 *Midnight in the Century* is dedicated to several comrades, some dead, some in prison. Serge himself says, 'I dedicate these messages' to, Kurt Landau, Andres Nin, Erwin Wolf; to Joaquin Maurin in prison, and to Juan Andrade, Julian Gorkin, Katia Landau and Olga Nin. Andres Nin, one of the leaders of the POUM, kidnapped and murdered in Spain in June 1937 by Stalinist agents, was a hugely important figure also to George Orwell, who had served with a POUM brigade in Spain. In his classic biography, Bernard Crick states, 'The memory of the martyred Nin stayed with Orwell', and the 'hate' figure of Goldstein in *Nineteen Eighty-Four* 'is Nin quite as much as Trotsky'; much of his testimony in the novel derives from pamphlets in Orwell's possession by, or about, Nin, rather than from Trotsky, as is usually assumed. (*George Orwell: a life*, Penguin Books, 1992, pp. 227, 365).

13 A vivid account of Serge's expulsion from Russia, the theft of his poetry and other papers, and the hopeful search for them after the opening up of the Soviet Union, is given by Murray Armstrong in 'The searchers', *Guardian*, 22 September 1990.

14 These were helpfully brought together by Al Richardson in *Collected Writings on Literature and Revolution*, 2004.

15 Kolyma, an area of north-eastern Siberia, was a source of gold and a vast prison camp. It was administered by a trust, Far Northern Construction, set up by the Soviet state in 1931 to run forced labor in the area. The FNC expanded and may well have been running a prison camp the size of the whole of Western Europe. As many as three million people may have died there - from the cold, hunger, exhaustion, brutality. (Shalamov was asked by Solzhenitsyn to collaborate on *The Gulag Archipelago* but declined because of his

age.) He died in 1982. (See John Glad's 'Foreword', to his translation of the stories, Penguin, 1994.)

16 The best introduction to the art of the period remains Camilla Gray's pioneering, *The Russian Experiment in Art, 1863-1922*, revised after her untimely death by Marian Burleigh-Motley, Thames and Hudson, 1962/1986. See also Norbert Lynton, *Tatlin's Tower: monument to revolution*, Yale University Press, 2009, and Victor Margolin, *The Struggle for Utopia: Rodchenko, Lissitzy, Moholy=Nagy, 1917-1946*, University of Chicago Press, 1997. For a different level of analysis from a radical perspective, see TJ Clark, *Farewell to an Idea; episodes in the history of modernism* (Yale University Press, 1999), especially Chapter 5, 'God is not cast down'.

17 The only instance I have come across of Serge writing about visual art was when he was in Berlin as a Comintern agent and went to the autumn exhibition of the Academy of Fine Art, where he found nothing but torment, suffering and darkness, and artists, including Barlach, Kollwitz and Kokoschka, who know 'nothing of joy'; it was, he said, the 'decadent art of a dying civilization' (*Witness to the German Revolution*, pp. 257-8).

18 Eisenstein himself admired the writing of Charles Olson, whose words I've used as the epigraph, although he did not live to see this poem.

19 Strangely, the avant-garde film-maker, Maya Deren, who was born in Russia in 1917, did her own translation of Serge's *Conquered City*. It was found in her papers after she died tragically in 1961 at the age of 41.

20 An architect of a different kind, Berthold Lubetkin, eventually found himself in London where his work continues quietly to astonish. Born in 1901, the son of a railroad engineer who would be murdered in Auschwitz, Lubetkin had been a student of the Vkhutemas, where his teachers included Rodchenko and Tatlin, and later at

Svomas in Petrograd. A reservist in the Red Army during the civil war, he had designed the USSR Trades Pavilion used at various locations in Europe in the late 20s. In 1932, he set up his practice, Tecton, which would last until 1948. Lubetkin may be best known for his 1934 penguin pool at London Zoo, but his Highpoint flats in north London continue to stun, especially on a bright day; they were praised by Le Corbusier himself, as 'an achievement of the first rank'. But Lubetkin was aware of the contradiction he found himself in, designing housing for middle class intellectuals. (The original brief by Zigmund Gestetner had been for a building to house his employees at his north London factory. Apart from its successor, Highpoint Two, Tecton would only build public buildings.) In 1935, Tecton was commissioned to build a health centre in the poor borough of Finsbury, in the heart of London; bringing together different facilities previously dispersed, the new centre would be, Lubetkin thought, a 'megaphone for health'. The building was poorly looked after, but continues in use, and is impressive still, as is Tecton's public housing, for instance the Hallfield Estate, near London's Paddington Station, living testimony to a belief in good quality housing, that is also architecturally innovative. They are, in architectural historian John Allan's beautiful summation, 'buildings that cry out for a world that has never come into being'.

After the war, Lubetkin agreed to be the architect/planner for Peterlee, near Durham, one of the new towns being built as part of the reconstruction after the devastations of the war. But two years of opposition to his innovative ideas, and incessant bureaucratic wrangling, left him defeated. and eventually he resigned. The town was then built on the more usual lines of anonymous urban sprawl. He went into semi-retirement, but still was involved in new work and in teaching, before his death in 1990. (See Malcolm Reading and

Peter Coe, *Lubetkin and Tecton: an architectural study*, Triangle Architectural Publishing, 1992).

21 My copy of *Destiny of a Revolution* was published by Hutchinson, along with something called the National Book Association and looks, at first sight, like one of those classic Left Book Club editions of the 1930s. It carries a printed leaflet by Arthur Bryant, a popular historian, who became an admirer of Hitler and the Nazis. (Two years after they published Serge, they published a new version of Hitler's *Mein Kampf!*) Bryant says Serge is an 'unrepentant Communist', who fails to see that what he describes is the 'inevitable result of applying the Marxian doctrine to the real world'. (Even he praises Serge for 'lucidly and dispassionately' portraying the details of life in Russia: 'Not Dante himself painted such a picture of horror and inhumanity as this lifelong Communist'.) Bryant's corrective is necessary because there is not one word in the book that justifies its use as right-wing propaganda. Bryant was also involved in the Right Book Club, set up in 1937 by WA Foyle, owner of the prestigious London bookshop, and actively led by his daughter, the autocratic Christina who, infamously, never allowed trade unions in the shop.

22 'The art of interpreting nonexistent inscriptions written in invisible ink on a blank page' in Simon Leys, *The Angel and the Octopus: collected essays and articles 1983-1999*, Duffy and Snellgrove, 1999, and *Chinese Shadows*, Penguin, 1978.

23 Dan Gretton, and others from Platform, the political arts organization, inspired by Semprun's book, walked from Goethe's house in Weimar to Buchenwald: 'the distance from humanism to barbarism is 10,166 steps'. Semprun's memoir, *Literature or Life* (1997), also begins at Buchenwald on the day of its liberation. Semprun, who has not had a mirror for years, sees himself reflected in the faces of his British liberators, 'in that terror-stricken gaze, I see myself - in their

horror'.

24 The English translation was published with the title, *Communism in Spain in the Franco Era*, which makes it sound like a politics text-book, which it most certainly is not.

25 See the obituary by Michael Eaude, *Guardian* 20 June 2011. Semprun also wrote the compelling and sophisticated novel of political intrigue, *The Second Death of Ramon Mercader* (1973), as well as others never translated into English.

26 An article by Fraenckel and Lennhof, 'On the psychology of National Socialism', (translated by Eileen Holly and Ursula Ott), was published in *Free Associations*, 2002, pp. 216 - 226.

27 Bettelheim's article was first published in Dwight Macdonald's journal, *Politics*, to which Serge was also a contributor. He incorporated it into his classic book, *The Informed Heart* (1960).

28 Fromm's book was published in Britain in 1942 as *The Fear of Freedom*. A later book, *Marx's Concept of Man* (1961), making use of Marx's early writings, in particular the 'Economic and philosophical manuscripts', helped bring the humanist Marx to a wide audience.

Contemporary culture has eliminated both the concept of the public and the figure of the intellectual. Former public spaces – both physical and cultural – are now either derelict or colonized by advertising. A cretinous anti-intellectualism presides, cheerled by expensively educated hacks in the pay of multinational corporations who reassure their bored readers that there is no need to rouse themselves from their interpassive stupor. The informal censorship internalized and propagated by the cultural workers of late capitalism generates a banal conformity that the propaganda chiefs of Stalinism could only ever have dreamt of imposing. Zer0 Books knows that another kind of discourse – intellectual without being academic, popular without being populist – is not only possible: it is already flourishing, in the regions beyond the striplit malls of so-called mass media and the neurotically bureaucratic halls of the academy. Zer0 is committed to the idea of publishing as a making public of the intellectual. It is convinced that in the unthinking, blandly consensual culture in which we live, critical and engaged theoretical reflection is more important than ever before.